# LADDERS AND SHOVELS

# HOW TO CLIMB OUT OF EMOTIONAL HOLES AND STOP DIGGING THEM

Christian J. Dean, Ph.D.

First Published 2022 by Flamenco Media, LLC
Baton Rouge, LA

All rights reserved. No part of this book may be reprinted or reproduced or utilized in any form or by any electronic, mechanical, or other means, now known or hereafter invented, including photocopying and recording, or in any information storage or retrieval system, without permission in writing from the publisher.

Copyright © 2022 Christian J. Dean

All rights reserved.

ISBN: 979-8-9870134-0-3

# DEDICATION

To my clients: past, present, and future.

# TABLE OF CONTENTS

INTRODUCTION ............................................................................... 1
CHAPTER 1: AN OVERVIEW OF LADDERS, SHOVELS AND COGNITIVE-BEHAVIORAL CONCEPTS ....................................... 3
CHAPTER 2: COMMON FEELINGS AND SHOVEL THOUGHTS ...................................................................................... 25
CHAPTER 3: COMMON SHOVEL THOUGHTS ......................... 32
CHAPTER 4: BUILDING LADDER THOUGHTS ....................... 51
CHAPTER 5: EMOTIONAL MATH .................................................. 67
CHAPTER 6: FORGIVENESS ............................................................. 71
CHAPTER 7: PERSONAL ADJUSTMENTS AND SUPPLEMENTAL METAPHORS ....................................................... 75
CHAPTER 8: PUTTING IT ALL TOGETHER ............................... 79
APPENDIX A: HELPFUL TOOLS AND RESOURCES .............. 83
ABOUT THE AUTHOR ........................................................................ 91

# ACKNOWLEDGMENTS

A heartfelt thank you to my wife and love of my life, Kelly. Your support, love, and encouragement push me to be a better husband and father every day. Thank you for reading the drafts, providing your thoughts, making suggestions on every aspect of the book, and listening to my ideas. Your support and love mean the world to me.

A heartfelt thank you to my children, Sydney and Christian, Jr. who tolerate my "therapizing" personality and who, along with their mother, brighten my life every day.

A heartfelt thank you to my mother, Cristina and my late father, Jackie. Your guidance, support, and love throughout my life has helped me tremendously.

# INTRODUCTION

Benjamin Franklin is often quoted for his famous words *"…in this world, nothing is certain except death and taxes."* I would like to add that some form of adversity, challenge, or distress is also a certainty in life. These challenges may be associated with many different things, such as heartbreak, other relationship difficulties, financial distress, devastating natural or manmade disasters, physical disabilities, or emotional/mental health distress. Throughout my time as a mental health professional working with children, adolescents, adults, couples, and family systems, I have realized that the distress caused by mental health factors can be extremely debilitating. The purpose of this book is to provide the reader with some tools to assist with reducing emotional distress while also helping to overcome obstacles and challenges. The intent is not to diagnose or to replace therapy or counseling services that is needed or being received. Instead, the intent is to provide the reader with resources and an approach to increase emotional well-being.

## Challenging Times

Beth was a 24-year-old accountant who found out her fiancé, Brad, was unfaithful to her. She was understandably upset about the discovery and felt betrayed by the man she loved. She was willing to forgive Brad, but he decided to end the relationship and call off the wedding. Beth was devastated when Brad moved out. She started questioning her self-worth. Thoughts popped into her mind even though she tried to block them. These were not just thoughts that led her to feel sad about missing Brad or having her dreams of marrying him crushed. These thoughts were also about her self-worth. Thoughts like "you are no good," "no one will ever marry you" and "men cannot be trusted" flushed her mind.

Beth is not alone in her experiences. Many of us confront challenging situations that make life difficult. Unfortunately, these challenging times may be accompanied by automatic thoughts that disrupt our sense of self and overall well-being (later referred to as Shovel Thoughts). In Beth's case, we can see the all-or-nothing type of theme of "no" and "never." Beth is not necessarily choosing to have these thoughts as they are automatic; however, she can learn to: 1) **D**issect them to see if they are rational or have a basis of support; 2) **E**valuate the Value of whether focusing and thinking of things this way is worth the emotional toll they have on her and if it is in her best interest to believe them; and 3) **W**eigh the support of continuing to entertain or believe these thoughts. The **D.E.W.** acronym will be further explored to reinforce the three main Ladder Thoughts that will help us climb out of emotional holes.

**What to Expect**

The following chapters provide an overview and detailed examples of thought processes that result in individuals digging themselves into emotional holes. More importantly, we will offer detailed "how-to" instructions on the process for climbing out of the holes and learning not to dig them. All too often, I've heard clients ask, "But how can I change my thought patterns?" Well, this book will provide some guidance on that process. The first chapter will provide an initial foundation for understanding how our thoughts, feelings and behaviors are all connected. Chapters 2 and 3 will cover common Shovel Thought processes we all tend to experience from time to time. Chapter 4 will provide detailed information on how to construct Ladder Thoughts to help you overcome emotional obstacles or dig yourselves out of emotional holes. Chapters 5 and 6 will provide additional concepts to aid in the process of establishing healthy thought processes and outlooks. Finally, Chapters 7 and 8 will provide the application of Ladder Thoughts as well as other metaphors or analogies that may be helpful in conceptualizing ways to improve overall emotional well-being.

# CHAPTER 1

# AN OVERVIEW OF LADDERS, SHOVELS AND COGNITIVE-BEHAVIORAL CONCEPTS

Imagine that the journey of life is like a road. Throughout our lives, we take different turns on the road as we explore our goals, desired destinations and companionship for this journey. As we travel down this road, we may encounter some barriers that get in the way, slow us down or interrupt our progress. These barriers are the challenges in life that we all experience from time to time. These challenges may be something as simple as traffic or as tragic as the death of a loved one. Challenges can also be unique to each individual.

When we encounter these barriers, we have two main choices on how to react. The choices are 1) grabbing a shovel and digging ourselves into a hole by thinking in ways that negatively impact our emotional well-being, or 2) grabbing a ladder to climb over the barrier and moving forward by using thought-changing processes. Many times, our reactions are almost automatic, without conscious thought (remember Beth in the introduction).

Choice 1, digging ourselves into a hole, often happens automatically due to social and cognitive conditioning. Many people think negatively about circumstances in their lives, then automatically, without conscious awareness, they pick up the shovel to start digging. These barriers may sometimes be a thought itself, a negative Shovel Thought that results in automatic digging. These Shovel Thoughts are often subconscious, and we reach for them to our detriment. Shovel Thoughts result in an additional obstacle in our journey of life.

# LADDERS AND SHOVELS

The additional obstacle is that we now must climb out of the emotional hole we have dug before we can even climb over the obstacle in our way.

In Chapter 2, we will cover the various forms of Shovel Thoughts and identify different thought patterns and themes that tend to be present in many of us.

Choice 2, grabbing a ladder and climbing over the obstacle, can also happen in multiple ways; however, we often benefit from fighting the subconscious and automatic urges to grab the shovel.

Ladder Thoughts are more productive and focused thoughts that help us climb out of emotional holes that were dug by Shovel Thoughts. Ladder Thoughts also help us climb over barriers that arise from challenges in our lives. At times, we will have to construct our Ladder Thoughts rung-by-rung while working on dissecting and deconstructing the Shovel Thoughts. Chapter 4 will cover methods to develop and construct Ladder Thoughts to be used, if chosen, throughout the rest of our lives. To highlight the power of thoughts, I want to quote Mahatma Gandhi, who said: *"A man is but the product of his thoughts. What he thinks, he becomes."*

# LADDERS AND SHOVELS

## Cognitive-Behavioral Foundation

The concept of Ladder and Shovel Thoughts is based on the Cognitive-Behavioral Theory of human emotions and behaviors. When implemented in therapy, it is often called Cognitive-Behavioral Therapy (or CBT). The concepts behind CBT will be demonstrated below in a scenario that you can process. Think of someone who you may go on a date with, hang out with, or who may just give you a ride. Once you have someone in mind, write down their name in the (name) blank below and follow the instructions.

### *Scenario:*

It is 5:00 p.m. and _____ (Insert name of person) was supposed to pick you up at 4:30 p.m. You call their cellphone, and it goes straight to voice mail. At this time, how would you feel? Fill in the blank with a feeling word (e.g., worried, angry, sad, excited, happy, relieved, frustrated, etc.).

*Step 1)*

I felt: _____

What thought did you have that led you to feel that way? Fill in the blank.

I thought:

_____

_____

What would your next action be if you thought and felt that way? Fill in the blank.

I would:

_____

_____

*Step 2)*

What could be another possible reason why they have not yet picked you up?

_____

_____

If you had thought that instead of your first thought, would you feel any differently? (yes or no) _____

If yes, what would you feel instead?

_____

If you felt differently, would you have changed your actions? (yes or no) _____

If yes, what would you have done differently? _____

_____

*Step 3)*

Did you notice any difference in your emotional reaction (feeling) based on a different thought? (yes or no) _____ If so, great! If not, great! It is just an exercise.

If you did not notice any difference, let me present some potential responses:

    1) If I thought "They must have forgotten about me," then I would most likely feel disappointed, and my behavior may be to call and leave a message expressing that disappointment.

    2) If I thought "They must be in traffic," then I would most likely feel content, and I may patiently wait as I can relate to traffic delays.

    3) If I thought "They may have gotten into an accident," then I would most likely feel worried or anxious, and I may call and leave a message simply asking them to let me know that they are safe.

**THE POINT OF THE EXERCISE:** We can be presented with the same situation, and our emotional reactions to that situation (e.g., how we feel) will depend on how we think about it, which will directly impact how we behave in response to the feeling. In the responses provided above, we see that there were three varying thoughts resulting in three different feelings and three different behaviors. Again, it is not what happens but how you think about it that leads you to feel the way you do.

Another view of the example:

1)
   a) Thought = He must have forgotten about me.
      ↓
   b) Feeling = Disappointment.
      ↓
   c) Behavior = Calling the person and saying, "Where are you? Don't you know you were supposed to pick me up?"

2)
   a) Thought = He must be in traffic.
      ↓
   b) Feeling = content.
      ↓
   c) Behavior = Patiently waiting.

3)
   a) Thought = He may have gotten in an accident.
      ↓
   b) Feeling = Worried.
      ↓
   c) Behavior = Calling the person and asking if they are safe.

## Definitions of Emotions/Feelings

The following definitions of emotions are being provided to establish some common understanding of what these emotions may mean or look like. The intent with these definitions is to help the reader better connect the most accurate core (or initial) emotion that is present versus focusing on a secondary emotion. For example, sometimes we may feel frustrated, and, if we are not careful, the feeling of frustration can turn to anger. So, we want to stop ourselves when we feel frustrated so that it doesn't escalate to anger. We can work on adjusting our emotions when they are more intense, but it is much easier to change our less intense emotions. Therefore, identifying that "core feeling" first can be helpful to this process.

Consider the following scenario: If I trip and someone laughs, I may feel embarrassed. Now, if I'm not careful, I may externalize that embarrassment and become angry with the person who laughed and think, "You shouldn't laugh at people. I could have gotten hurt. I'll give you something to laugh about." Or I may internalize it and become angry with myself when I think, "No one likes me. I'm such an idiot. I can't even walk without making a fool of myself." Or I may internalize it and become anxious, "I'd better be careful or I'm going to trip again. Am I going to trip again? I hope I don't trip again. I need to watch where I'm going." The milder feeling of embarrassment is easier to manage than the more intense feelings of anger or anxiety. This example demonstrates how it is not *what happens* but *how we think about it* that leads us to feel (and then act) a certain way. When feeling embarrassed, it is often helpful to remember that we are human, and we all make mistakes or have accidents. We might also want to consider that we also might have an initial urge to laugh at others that when they trip. I find a lot of value in working on not taking things personally when someone laughs at me for something that may seem funny to them.

Many people may misinterpret their emotional state due to past experiences. Consider the case of Robert, who responds in anger to his wife after she pulls away from him when he tries to hug her. Initially, Robert is probably not angry. Instead, Robert's initial emotional reaction was hurt. Shovel Thoughts are what usually change the emotion from hurt to anger.

Your definition of these emotions may be different, which is fine. Please feel free to use or identify with the emotional definition that best fits your understanding.

**Stress:** "The pattern of specific and non-specific responses a person makes to stimulus events that disturb his or her equilibrium and tax or exceed his or her ability to cope" (American Psychiatric Association [APA], 2013, p. 829). I think of stress as pressured responses to things in life. For example, if I forgot about an appointment, I may feel stress if my goal is to get to the appointment on time. However, someone could think to themselves *forget the appointment*, and the situation may not lead to stress. When I reflect on the definition of stress, the key component for me is the question of what will disturb me. If I work on not allowing things to disturb me, then maybe I can reduce the frequency or severity of any perceived stress.

**Stressor:** "Any emotional, physical, social, economic, or other factor that disrupts the normal physiological, cognitive, emotional, or behavioral balance of an individual" (APA, 2013, p. 829). Based on the earlier scenario, the stressor would have been forgetting about the appointment. Stressors come in different forms, and what may be a stressor to one person may not be a big deal to another.

**Worry:** "Unpleasant or uncomfortable thoughts that cannot be consciously controlled by trying to turn the attention to other subjects. The worrying is often persistent, repetitive, and out of proportion to the topic worried about (it can even be about a triviality)" (APA, 2013, p. 831). Based on the definition, we can clearly see that worry is significantly, if not entirely, associated with thoughts. Recognizing the thoughts that trigger the emotions and focusing on ways to challenge the thoughts is the premise of the book. Turning our attention to something else is usually not enough to help. Therefore, constructing Ladder Thoughts is the recommended method to address the Shovel Thoughts that result from feeling worried.

**Anxiety:** "The apprehensive anticipation of future danger or misfortune accompanied by a feeling of worry, distress, and/or somatic symptoms of tension. The focus of anticipated danger may be internal or external" (APA, 2013, p. 818).

Another way to think about anxiety is to consider when the worrisome thoughts (unpleasant or uncomfortable) focus on the occurrence of future danger or misfortune. I want to point out the significant difference between worry and anxiety. I may worry that I have forgotten to pay the rent; however, it turns into anxiety when I then think, *Because I did not pay, I'll get evicted, and have to live on the streets where I will die.* The shift from worry to anxiety happens when we take it to that level of danger or misfortune.

**Fear:** "An emotional response to perceived imminent threat or danger associated with urges to flee or fight" (APA, 2013, p. 821). Different from worry and anxiety, fear prepares the body to react, and it is in response to a perceived threat or danger. In worry and anxiety, the unpleasant or uncomfortable thoughts, or the apprehensive anticipation of the potential danger or misfortune, are often about what could happen in the future. With fear, it is more of an immediate response because the individual perceives the threat or danger to be imminent.

**Anger:** A common and at times unsettling emotion, anger can be triggered by many thoughts. A definition of anger includes: "a strong feeling of displeasure and usually of antagonism" (Merriam-Webster, n.d.). This definition highlights the components of displeasure and antagonism. Antagonism is defined as "active hostility or opposition" (Merriam-Webster, n.d.). Therefore, the displeasure is then expressed or focused on active hostility or opposition. I often think of the quote from Charles Eads, *"Hurt people hurt people,"* and how anger is often a secondary emotion that becomes externalized onto others but originates in our own hurt, displeasure, etc.

**Disgust:** Disgust is defined as: "marked aversion aroused by something highly distasteful" and to be disgusting (Verb) is "to provoke to loathing, repugnance, or aversion: be offensive to" (Merriam-Webster, n.d.). I'm sure we have all seen or eaten something that we have considered disgusting. When it comes to interpersonal interactions and relationships, disgust is a very concerning emotion. If we feel disgust toward someone or something they did, it can be problematic due to the potential intensity of this emotion.

**Contempt:** Like disgust, contempt can be a very strong emotion. Contempt is defined as: "the act of despising: the state of mind of one who despises" or "lack of respect or reverence for something" (Merriam-Webster, n.d.). Contempt, like disgust, can make interpersonal interactions and relationships difficult.

**Jealous:** There are several definitions of the word jealous: a) "hostile toward a rival or one believed to enjoy an advantage"; b) "intolerant of rivalry or unfaithfulness"; c) "disposed to suspect rivalry or unfaithfulness" (Merriam-Webster, n.d.). Feelings of jealousy can arise from different contexts and may be associated with a romantic interest or partner, vehicles (what kind a car someone drives) and reputation or fame, among other things.

**Defeated:** The definition that I want to highlight for defeated is: "frustration by nullification or by prevention of success" (Merriam-Webster, n.d.). In my opinion, this definition highlights the essence of the emotion being related to a shift from frustration to a sense of wanting to stop trying and giving up.

**Sad:** Merriam-Webster (n.d.) defines sad as: "affected with or expressive of grief or unhappiness" (Merriam-Webster, n.d.). However, I would caution you to consider this to be a misleading definition. The inclusion of not being affected by happiness does not necessarily mean that an individual would be sad. There are many other emotions that include frustration, disappointment or content. This is one of the reasons I encourage people to understand different emotions and be able to differentiate them. Sadness can include difficulty with feeling other neutral or positive emotions. Concepts like feeling down can often be associated with feeling sad.

**Overwhelmed:** This is an emotion that I hear being expressed a lot in the past several years. To be overwhelmed means: "completely overcome or overpowered by thought or feeling" (Merriam-Webster, n.d.). I do find this definition interesting since the focus is not on tasks or activities. Often, people express feeling overwhelmed due to things they think they must do or tasks they must complete. However, the thoughts and feelings behind the tasks are at the core of the concept of feeling overwhelmed.

**Frustrated:** I find that frustration is a common core emotion that people probably experience before it turns into more intense emotions like anger. Frustration is defined as: "a deep chronic sense or state of insecurity and dissatisfaction arising from unresolved problems or unfulfilled needs" (Merriam-Webster, n.d.). I want to highlight the focus on unresolved problems or unfulfilled needs as the main component of what makes frustration different from other emotions. When working through some of the exercises in this book, ask yourself, "Is there a problem that is not being resolved, or is there a need that is not being fulfilled"? Such questions can help us better identify the emotion that may initially be present.

**Guilty:** Guilt is defined as: "a feeling of deserving blame for offenses" and "feelings of deserving blame especially for imagined offenses or from a sense of inadequacy" (Merriam-Webster, n.d.). I want to point out the key components of blame and offenses. I often find that individuals feel guilt over things that they are not responsible for (i.e., they did not do anything to hurt or offend someone). At times, this may be due to someone else trying to convince them that was their fault; in fact, it is almost always not their responsibility.

**Betrayed:** I believe it would first be helpful to understand what the word "betray" means. To betray, the verb or action, has several meanings: "to lead astray" or "to fail or desert especially in time of need" or "to disclose in violation of confidence" (Merriam-Webster, n.d.). Betrayed, on the other hand, is: "treacherously abandoned, deserted, or mistreated" (Merriam-Webster, n.d.). The addition of "treacherously" is somewhat concerning; however, it may help to highlight how powerful betrayal is in terms of emotional intensity.

**Disappointed:** Like betrayed, I believe it would first be helpful to understand what it means "to disappoint" before getting to the definition of disappointed. To disappoint is: "to fail to meet the expectation or hope of" (Merriam-Webster, n.d.), and disappointed is: "defeated in expectation or hope" (Merriam-Webster, n.d.). We often feel disappointed (i.e., defeated in our expectation or hope of something happening or of someone doing something) when someone disappoints us (i.e., they don't follow through on what we expected them to do).

## The Process of Constructing Ladders and Deconstructing Shovels

The process of constructing Ladder Thoughts while deconstructing Shovel Thoughts will take some time to practice with the goal of continuous improvement. I suggest getting a journal and writing down your responses to each step of the process. I also suggest that you bookmark this section for easy reference when using this guide. Let's walk through the process step-by-step so you can learn to use this in your daily life.

*1. Write down what happened.*

Write down the events that led you to start feeling an emotion that you would not want to feel (e.g., anger, sadness, depression, frustration, disappointment, etc.)

One scenario may be: "Someone is cheating in a game, and I start to feel _____." I know I start to feel frustrated when someone is cheating in a game. I can also feel disappointed if the individual cheating demonstrated a behavior I would not expect of them. Additionally, remember that Shovel Thoughts may not necessarily be related to a specific event but just to a random thought that pops into your mind. In those instances, write down the thought and indicate that it just popped into your mind.

*2. Write down how you felt.*

Write down the feeling that you did not want to have (e.g., angry, sad, mad, depressed, frustrated, disappointed, embarrassed, scared, worried, etc.). Think about what the first feeling (i.e., the core emotion) was.

*3. Write down your Shovel Thought(s).*

Shovel Thoughts are the thoughts that lead us to feel angry, sad, worried, frustrated, depressed, disappointed, embarrassed, scared, etc. Almost everyone experiences Shovel Thoughts from time to time.

These thoughts and thought patterns are referred to as Shovel Thoughts because they dig us into emotional holes, making it even harder to overcome the challenge or barrier. These thoughts are often automatic and pop up in our minds even when we may not want them to.

We want to write down the specific Shovel Thought and the resulting emotional reaction. We will get more into what the Shovel Thoughts look like in detail later in the book. The section below will provide an overview.

**Shovel Thoughts**

Here are the different categories of Shovel Thoughts with some explanations:

a) Expectations and Entitlements – include "should" statements, thoughts that also include the words must, need, supposed to, ought to, etc., which can often have an entitlement component (e.g., I did this therefore you should…); they may also be externalized (i.e., pushed onto someone else) or internalized (i.e., pushed onto ourselves). When they are internalized, they become another form of Shovel Thoughts called <u>My Fault Thinking</u>. These Shovel Thoughts focus negative energy on us, beating ourselves up emotionally while taking on responsibility for many, most and occasionally all negative things that occur to self or others.

b) Blaming and Responsibility – often associated with an attempt to justify what we do or don't do, or putting the responsibility of our feelings or actions on someone else.

c) Worst-Case Thoughts – thinking of the worst-case scenario, which tends to be extreme.

d) "This Always Happens" *or* "Here We Go Again" – assuming that a situation will have the same result as in the past. We may see a behavior or hear something and think, "I knew it. Here we go again." At this point, we are not open to communication, and we are focused on the perceived or assumed upcoming argument or negative result.

e) All-or-Nothing Thinking – Looking at life from extremes

or absolutes is related to All-or-Nothing Thinking. When we say, "You *never* show me affection," is it really "never"? Probably not! However, this kind of thinking leads to extreme emotional reactions.

f) "And Then..." Thinking – Seeing life as having a negative domino effect (i.e., this bad thing is going to happen, and then this, and then that and then the other), resulting in a sequence of negative thoughts. Such sequences usually result in emotional distress.

g) Body Messages – usually triggered by some form of physiological experience. Something our body does, or some form of physical sensation, will initiate the Shovel Thought, resulting in a spiraling thought-feeling-physical reaction cycle.

h) "What if..." – a tendency to focus on not-so-positive outcomes in our lives. They may not be as catastrophic as the Worst-Case Thoughts but can nonetheless cause a lot of distress.

Now, we all experience Shovel Thoughts in one way or another. Some may experience them more than others; however, if we get into an unhealthy habit of habitually thinking with Shovel Thoughts, t can interfere with our overall well-being. Future chapters in the book will go into more detail regarding the different kinds of Shovel Thoughts and how to challenge them with Ladder Thoughts to change the way you think, feel, and behave.

*4. Write down your Ladder Thought(s).*

These are the helpful processes I call Ladder Thoughts, that we use to challenge the Shovel Thoughts in order to shift our emotional state. To me, Ladder Thoughts help you reclaim your calm or contentment while reducing the amount of time we may feel angry, sad, worried, frustrated, depressed, disappointed, embarrassed, scared, etc. There are three different ways to implement and build a Ladder Thought, and the acronym **D.E.W.** will help you remember the steps. The **D** in **D.E.W.** stands for **D**issecting the method of building Ladder Thoughts; the **E.** stands for **E**valuate the Value method; and the **W** stands for **W**eighed Ladder Thought.

The following three points are brief introductions to the process of each type of Ladder Thought:

a) **D**issecting Ladder Thoughts – to use this method, write down a Ladder Thought that is directly related to the Shovel Thought and strong enough to overcome it (i.e., help us climb out of the hole and/or over the barrier). In this process, we dissect and break down the Shovel Thought piece-by-piece to challenge each aspect of the thought. We also develop a solution-focused approach with the Ladder Thought, if possible.

**D**issecting Ladder Thought:

Shovel Thought = They <u>should not</u> have cut me off.

Dissecting = Where is it written that people shouldn't cut me off? I may not like it, but I'm not immune from being cut off.

Ladder Thought = I <u>would like people not</u> to cut me off, but I can't control how they drive.

b) **E**valuate the Value Ladder Thoughts - my preferred way to use this method is to ask yourself some questions. For example: "How is thinking this way or feeling this way going to help anything? If thinking and/or feeling a certain way is not going to get things resolved, then it may not be in my best interest to continue thinking/feeling that way. What is the cost of thinking and feeling this way (emotional, physical, relational, etc.), and what is the payout or reward (what do I get out of it?) for thinking and feeling this way"? By asking ourselves these questions, we are determining if there is any positive value in our thoughts and emotional reactions.

c) **W**eighed Ladder Thoughts - this method focuses on weighing the facts and exploring what is more accurate. What facts (not opinions) support this thought, and what facts do not support this thought? We want to explore and weigh the facts that support the thought versus those that do not. If there are more facts that support the thought, then we want to shift the focus and apply the Emotional Math process found later in Chapter 5.

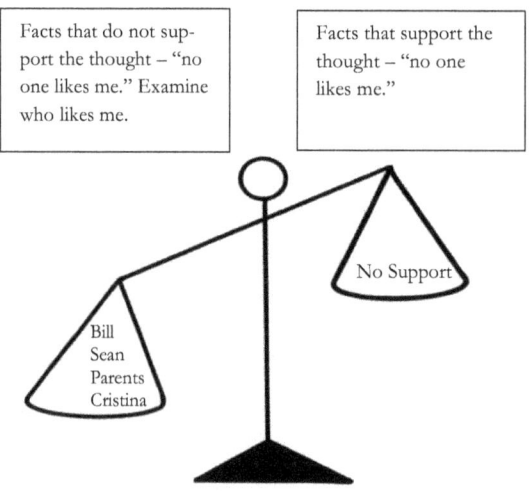

**W**eighed Ladder Thought

We can write down one or a combination of the processes involved in **D.E.W**. All Ladder Thought approaches have a solution-focused component that will provide a more powerful method. Throughout the book, different Ladder Thought applications will have their subtype identified. The following section will provide more details on aspects of Ladder Thoughts.

**Ladder Thoughts**

Developing Ladder Thoughts can be difficult for some, as they have gotten so accustomed to thinking in problematic ways through the automatic use of Shovel Thoughts. The three ways of working through a Ladder Thought that are identified in the previous section provide a great start. Other approaches can be used that are simpler but still very powerful: a) How is thinking or feeling this way going to help anything? And looking at the cost and payout for thinking and feeling a certain way (**Evaluate the Value**); and b) Exploring what facts support or do not support the thought (**Weighed**).

<u>Evaluate the Value: What is the benefit of thinking this way?</u> This thought-changing process simply involves examining how thinking or feeling this way is going to help anything. For example, let's say that your business was having a bad month. If you started thinking,

"What is going to happen if things don't change? I may lose my business and not have any income for my family." Thinking this way may lead someone to feel stressed or worried. So, the challenge would be to think, "How is thinking this way or feeling this way going to help me? Doing so is only going to cause me distress. What can I do about this situation?" Once you have asked yourself these questions, then focus on actions you can take to address the situation (i.e., the behaviors). Identifying the actions/behaviors can include, "I can explore marketing strategies, perhaps some contract work, looking at getting a part-time job to supplement my income or exploring an emergency fund for the business." Consider how shifting the thinking and then focusing on solutions that may be actionable are more helpful than just worrying about it.

**W**eighed Ladder Thoughts: This approach is a form of the CBT process discussed in Chapter 1 and includes exploring what information or facts support the thought and exploring which ones do not support the thought. If the Shovel Thought was, "No one likes me," then the process would go as follows:

*Support for the thought*, "No one likes me": I know that some people do like me, so there is no support for this extreme thought.

*Support against the thought*, "No one likes me": Does anyone like me? Yes. Who? My friend Bill, my sister Cristina, my parents and my coworker, Sean, all like me. We get along, talk, have lunch and get together frequently. Therefore, there is support against the thought "no one likes me," and I will do this to change my thinking.

What if the support were in favor of the thought? What if one found more support for the thought "No one likes me?" I may then ask myself some questions: a) Do I want people to like me? b) Do I want to accept who I am? c) Do I want to focus on finding people who will like who I am already? I could also focus on solutions that may potentially help me change my actions/behaviors to increase the chances that people will like me: "What can I do to get along with people better and increase the chance that people will like me?" Once you've identified what actions/behaviors can be taken, then you can implement the changes needed. Action is important to change. Without taking some form of action in terms of changing our thoughts and behaviors, then it would be difficult to change the outcome of our emotional state. These steps are not easy; in fact, they take a lot of work.

Consider this process as any other self-help instruction manual or book. I can read a book or manual on personal finance, physical health and exercise, interpersonal relationships, etc., but I'll never get my finances, physical health or interpersonal relationship to be as healthy as I would like them to be unless I apply the principles in those books.

## Thoughts Versus Beliefs

An unfortunate reality of life is that we can't necessarily control every thought that pops into our minds. Thoughts sometimes just arise, even if we don't want them. We can, however, adjust or change our thought processes. However, this is much easier for thoughts than it is for beliefs. When we believe something, then we have accepted it as a fact or as truth. Thoughts associated with our beliefs will take much more work to challenge, adjust, and change. We can work on thoughts and beliefs as Chapter 5 will address Emotional Math as a process to help with beliefs.

## The Brain

In order to highlight the importance of writing down the Shovel Thoughts and Ladder Thoughts, I want to mention Dr. Dan Siegel's concept of "name it to tame it" as well as one of his explanations of the brain (see the video of Dr. Siegel's on YouTube titled "Name it to Tame it") (Dalai Lama Center for Peace and Education, 2014). In this short video, Dr. Siegel explains how the cortex (or what he calls the "upstairs brain") and the subcortex (or what he calls the "downstairs brain," which includes the limbic system and the brain stem) work. Dr. Siegel goes on to explain how naming the emotion can produce calming neurotransmitters when the amygdala (part of the limbic system) is hyperaroused (emotional). Dr. Seigel demonstrates how fear was the core emotion that was causing the amygdala to be hyperaroused, although the individual thought that the main emotion was anger.

The writing down of Shovel Thoughts and reflecting on the core emotion engages your cortex to help you not only "name it to tame it" but also helps you shift into the Ladder Thoughts-building process. Reflecting on the steps outlined in this chapter will help you engage your cortex more often and work on calming down versus staying in an emotionally hyperaroused state.

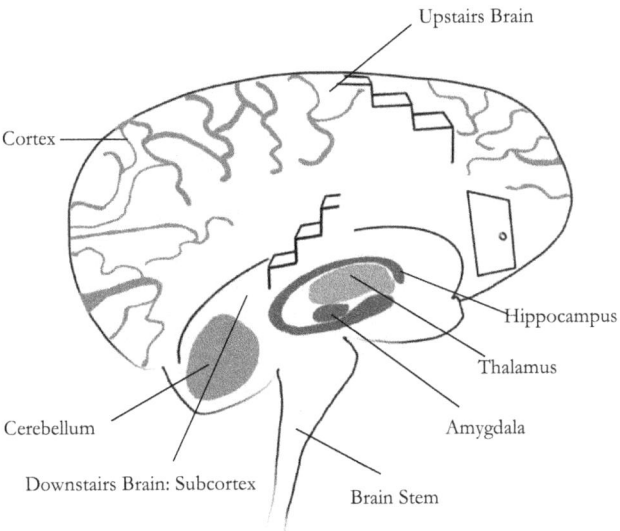

## Summary

Now that the foundation of the Shovel and Ladder Thought processes have been established, we can explore more specifics. Given the challenge of climbing out of emotional holes dug by Shovel Thoughts, the next chapter will focus on identifying the different types of Shovel Thoughts to increase awareness and understanding that will help you in the application of CBT. Such increased awareness and understanding are often helpful in choosing not to pick up the Shovel and to stop or reduce the digging process. I recognize that individuals may prefer other metaphors than the Ladders and Shovels identified. If so, you have an invitation to jump to Chapter 7 to explore other metaphors that may fit better to your situation. If you find one that makes more sense, consider replacing Ladders and Shovels with the preferred metaphor throughout the book.

## Homework

Take the time to identify some areas that you want to work on in terms of your thought processes and emotional state. Buy a notebook to be used as your journal for this process and to accompany you on this journey of reading this book. In your journal, write down thoughts that come to mind as you read and consider any insights or connections that you may find. Remember, just like anything in life, to be successful at change one must apply and practice what they are working toward. Use your journal to help reinforce the information in this book as a representation of your work toward change.

## References

American Psychiatric Association. (2013). *Diagnostic and statistical manual of mental disorders* (5th ed.). https://doi.org/10.1176/appi.books.9780890425596

Dalai Lama Center for Peace and Education. (2014, December 8). *Dan Siegel: Name it to tame it* [Video]. YouTube. https://www.youtube.com/watch?v=ZcDLzppD4Jc

Merriam-Webster. (n.d.). Merriam-Webster.com dictionary. Retrieved September 1, 2020, from https://www.merriam-webster.com/

# CHAPTER 2

# COMMON FEELINGS AND SHOVEL THOUGHTS

The early identification of the Shovel Thought-Feeling connection is important as it allows you to recognize when you *start* to dig emotional holes. Learning to identify these thoughts and feelings early on is essential to improving our emotions and interpersonal relationships. This chapter is not an all-inclusive list, but it provides some understanding of what kinds of Shovel Thoughts may be associated with your emotional reactions, and it will help you identify your own responses when working through identifying the type of thoughts you have. You will see subsections of this chapter start with headings listing different emotional reactions along with an explanation of what kinds of Shovel Thoughts tend to elicit them. Some terms may be familiar, and others may not. Make sure to identify which Shovel Thought-Feeling connections you tend to have, and write them down in the *Feelings Worksheet* found in Appendix A.

**Disappointment, Hurt, Guilt, Shame, and Sadness**

Disappointment, hurt, guilt, shame, and sadness are normal, everyday emotions. Some situations are simply sad, regardless of the thought process. If someone passes away, then it is totally understandable to experience sad feelings. We would not consider this unhealthy or inappropriate. However, if the sadness continues to grow and consume the individual to the point that it is getting in the way of life (e.g., work, relationships, school, etc.), then it may be more complicated, requiring some sort of therapy or therapeutic process. In many instances, disappointment, hurt, guilt, and sadness are caused by Shovel Thoughts that trigger these emotional reactions. Shovel Thoughts like the My Fault Thinking and All-or-Nothing tend to contribute to the emotions in the section.

*My Fault Shovel Thoughts*: These thoughts tend to occur when we internalize expectations, and they can lead to feeling angry with oneself. Additionally, and probably more common, My Fault Shovel Thoughts can lead to feeling disappointed with oneself or even feeling guilt or shame. Here are some examples of how My Fault Shovel Thoughts can lead to feeling disappointment, guilt, shame, or sadness.

Disappointment:
- I should have known better than to have bought that. (Internalized expectation: emotionally beat oneself up).
- I should have told her about how I felt; now it is too late. (Internalized expectation: then worst-case).

Guilt:
- I'm responsible for making my partner unhappy.
- I should have helped, but now it is my fault that things are not working out. (Internalized expectation)
- It's my fault that things didn't work out.

*All-or-Nothing Shovel Thoughts*: These kinds of thoughts are thoughts of extremes. It is difficult to see the "middle" or "gray" as the view tends to be on either end of the spectrum. The difficulty with these thoughts is that, if I think in extremes, then I will feel in extremes. Words like "always" and "never" tend to be associated with All-or-Nothing thinking and can trigger many different feelings. The following Shovel Thoughts display how they can lead to feeling hurt, disappointment, guilt, and sadness.

Hurt:
- You never show me you love me.

Disappointment:
- You never show up on time.

Sadness and/or Hopelessness:
- No one will ever love me.

- All of my relationships end badly, so what is the point?

<u>Guilt:</u>
- I'm always causing problems.

**Worry and Anxiety**

Worry and anxiety can lead to general distress and/or relational struggles. It may be due to the anxious individual demanding that something happen a certain way or that certain action be taken to help alleviate their anxiety. Also, once someone feels worried or anxious, it is easy to "thought jump" and think in different ways that lead to frustration or anger.

*"And Then" (or) "What If" Shovel Thoughts*: These types of thoughts lead to a "negative emotional domino effect" process. In other words, one "And Then" Shovel Thought triggers a series of "And Then" Shovel Thoughts that continue to be triggered or knocked down like a stack of lined-up dominos. These thought patterns have one of two ways of arising. Sometimes, these two ways can end up combining in one's thought patterns. The "And Then" Shovel Thought pattern tends to build up from one thought to the other. The "What If" Shovel Thought process is more scenario-based and often starts with "What if…" The following internal dialogue highlights how these thoughts can lead to feeling anxious.

> a. He is going to be upset about the change of plans. *(and)* Then he is going to say that he is tired of all the inconsistencies. *(and)* Then he is going to say he is tired of me. *(and)* Then he is going to say that it is not worth it anymore. *(and)* Then he is going to end our relationship.

> b. She is going to think that I was cheating. *(and)* Then she is going to bring up other times that she thought I was cheating. *(and)* Then she is going to say how she feels that she cannot trust me and that she can't be in a relationship where she can't feel comfortable and trust her partner. *(and)* Then she is going to end our relationship.

In these two scenarios, the resulting anxiety puts the individual at risk of thought jumping. Thought jumping is when the fear of something bad happening will trigger a defensive reaction that brings up other emotion-producing Shovel Thoughts. Below is a scenario demonstrating this idea:

> a. He is going to be upset about the change of plans. *(and)* Then he is going to say that he is tired of all the inconsistencies. *(and)* Then he is going to say he is tired of me. *(and)* Then he is going to say that it is not worth it. *(and)* Then he is going to end our relationship. – (thought jumping) But that is not fair. He is not consistent all the time, and he has unrealistic expectations. Why *(expectation)* is it always *(All-or-Nothing)* a big deal when a plan changes? Why *(expectation)* is he so inflexible? He should *(expectation)* be more flexible and be willing to go with the flow instead of making every little change an issue.

We can see how thought jumping can lead to the emotion changing from the initial and resulting anxiety to defensiveness, hypervigilance, frustration, and possibly anger. Feeling defensive or hypervigilant can often result in an attack-oriented posture. This posture will often lead to comments that are geared to reduce responsibility and blame by projecting, bringing up or conjuring up mistakes or responsibility on the part of the other person involved. This thought jumping can happen so fast (and often subconsciously) that the individual may not even be aware of what is happening. This is one reason to implement the Ladder Thought process and write down anytime you feel something you don't want to feel. By consistently writing it down, you will increase your awareness of the thought jumping and be better prepared to develop Ladder Thoughts to counteract the Shovel Thoughts, resulting in a healthier outcome. Remember to write down the Shovel Thoughts you tend to have related to these feelings in the *Feelings Worksheet* in Appendix A.

<u>*A note on internalized experiences versus externalized projections:*</u> There is no doubt that most of us don't like negative emotions like sadness, anxiety, disappointment, etc. When we do experience these feelings, we tend to be very uncomfortable sitting in the emotion. Stagnating in

our own emotional hole can be very difficult, and one way we distract from the discomfort is by shifting our focus and externalizing responsibility by blaming someone else. At that point, we try to place the discomfort onto someone else and often become angry instead. Unfortunately, some of us may experience less internal distress from feeling angry versus feeling those negative emotions of sadness, anxiety, and disappointment. I believe that there is much more value in working through those core emotions versus complicating the matter and feeling anger toward someone, as this can result in an escalation of Shovel Thoughts and digging deeper emotional holes.

*Worst-Case Thinking*: These kinds of thoughts tend to bypass the domino effect and go straight to a catastrophic end. There is often a huge leap from the current situation to a horrific event or outcome. Scenarios a. and b. show how Worst-Case Thinking can lead to feeling anxious.

a. My boss sent me an e-mail saying that she wants to talk to me. *She wants to meet so that she can fire me in person.*

b. My husband called and said we need to make some time to talk tonight. *He is going to tell me that he wants to get a divorce.*

## Frustration and Anger

Frustration and anger tend to go hand-in-hand. Often, people will say that they are angry when, in reality, they initially feel frustrated. Reflect on the most recent time that you felt angry. What happened? What were you thinking? What was your first thought and first emotional reaction? Did you feel something else before you felt angry? Awareness is essential and can help reduce the amount of time you feel frustrated and/or angry.

*Expectations and Entitlements*: These thoughts tend to be riddled with certain type of words and statements like *should, supposed to, need*, etc. We hear them every day of our lives. We sometimes internalize the expectations (like in the case of My Fault Shovel Thoughts on page 20) and emotionally beat ourselves up. However, people often externalize the expectations. Frustration can be triggered by different Shovel Thoughts using expectation words like:

Frustration:
- *Why* did you pay the bills late again?

- *Why* can't you pay the bills on time?

- Come on, by now you *should* know that you are *supposed* to put those up.

- Weren't you *supposed* to pick Billy up today?

Frustration can very easily shift into anger. Many times, individuals may say that they feel angry when, in fact, their core emotion was really frustration. Anger is different in that there is usually a form of hostility or opposition that can be externalized, and the negative energy is focused on someone else.

Anger:
- They should not have cut me off.

- He should have dinner prepared by the time I get home.

## Summary

These examples provide a brief look at common thoughts and emotions. Remember that Shovel Thoughts can lead to many emotions that may not necessarily fit into the patterns identified in this section. Each person is unique and may have different types of emotional reactions to different thoughts. Consider exploring the thoughts tied to the original feeling to identify the source of the emotion. Be aware of the thought-jumping concept and how it applies to your thoughts and related emotions.

## Homework

Go back to complete the *Feelings Worksheet* in Appendix A and continue to reflect on these concepts in your journal. Look for patterns or themes that arise in completing the Feelings Worksheet to help you become better aware of the types of Shovel Thoughts you tend to have that lead to the specific emotions identified.

# CHAPTER 3

# COMMON SHOVEL THOUGHTS

This chapter provides more details regarding common Shovel Thoughts many people experience, often on a regular basis. As you read through this chapter, consider your life and the thought patterns you tend to have. Make notes on the Shovel Thoughts that you tend to have most often. I encourage everyone to take notes and reflect. Through thoughtful reflection of our thinking patterns, we can increase awareness to help start the process early and change our thinking. Please remember, these Shovel Thoughts are almost automatic. We can't necessarily eliminate these thoughts from our lives, but instead we can become aware of them so that we can challenge them while adjusting our thinking with Ladder Thoughts. Use this chapter as a reference for when you practice the D.E.W. process in the aforementioned and future chapters.

**Expectations and Entitlements**

Expectation and Entitlement Shovel Thoughts are very common. These Shovel Thoughts tend to result in feelings of disappointment, frustration, aggravation, and anger. While these thoughts can lead to other feelings, generally speaking, these aforementioned feelings are most commonly the result. When we think with the words *should, ought to, supposed to, must or need,* we are approaching situations from an expectational point of view. We think with these words (e.g., should, must, need, etc.) when we want someone to do what we want them to do or when we don't want someone to do something. Some situations that can evoke these thoughts may involve someone breaking a rule that you believe they *should* follow or children not doing what their parents tell them to do: "They *need* to listen to their parents."

## Internalizing and Externalizing

The expectations that we have can often be internalized as well as externalized. Thinking "I *should* not have taken that job" or "I *should* have called when I was running late" are both internalized expectation statements. Depending on your personality and the habit you have established regarding your thought patterns, you may be more prone to either internalizing or externalizing; however, many people do both.

*Externalizing.* Externalizing expectations focus the energy on others. For example, you are driving, and someone cuts you off. If you think with the Shovel Thought, "He *should* not have cut me off," then you will likely start to feel frustrated or angry. Sometimes these Shovel Thoughts compound, and we dig ourselves into a deeper hole by adding additional thoughts like, "Luckily, I was paying attention. That driver could have caused a horrible wreck, and people could have been injured. They really need to watch where they are going." Those additional Shovel Thoughts add fuel to the fire, resulting in more frustration or anger. We want to change that Shovel Thought to a Ladder Thought (**D**issecting), like, "I don't want people to cut me off, but I can't control how they drive. Therefore, I can either sit here and be angry, which is not going to stop people from cutting me off and only increase my distress, or I can accept the fact that people will try to cut me off from time to time and stay alert as I drive with this knowledge." Remembering what Marcus Aurelius said can also be helpful during such incidents: *"You have power over your mind - not outside events. Realize this, and you will find strength."*

Sometimes, the word *why* might turn out to be a *should* in disguise. This does not apply every time you use the word "why," but it can if it is expectational- or entitlement-based. Consider a scenario in which a son hits his sister. The parent may ask, "*Why* did you hit your sister?", which can really mean, "You know you SHOULD NOT hit your sister." The parent has an expectation for the child to follow the rule of not hitting their sister. Often, no matter what the excuse is, the parent will feel that it still did not warrant hitting and may still carry a consequence.

At times, the word "*how*" can also have an expectation twist to it. To highlight this point, let's say someone finds out that their best friend and business partner has been stealing from the company. The individual may ask, "*How* could you do that to me?" This question is often asked due to the individual not expecting their friend and business partner to steal from them, which is probably a reasonable expectation; however, getting stuck in such thought patterns can often bring about more distress.

Shovel Thoughts may also have an entitlement component, which can be seen in the following Shovel Thought: "I've been working overtime all week, so my partner *should* have dinner prepared since they get home two hours before I do." We want to change that Shovel Thought to a Ladder Thought (**D**issecting), like: "I would like them to have dinner prepared by the time I get home, but being upset about it will not magically make dinner appear. Maybe we can work out a system to have things set up, scheduled, and prepared ahead of time."

Expectations and entitlements can often be a part of life that we experience at home, work, school, in social organizations, and other situations. If we are not careful, these expectation and entitlement statements can lead to feelings of frustration, anger, disappointment, and sadness. These emotions are not necessarily bad, but they may lead to more interpersonal difficulties.

*Internalizing – Entitlements.* Like the earlier example in the section ("they *should* have dinner prepared"), entitlements can lead to difficulties in one's life. Other aspects of entitlement can include what one thinks one *should* receive, regardless of their work, contributions, or favors. Also, it can include things that one believes they *should not* have to do as they believe they have already done their part. Entitlement type thoughts are often associated with things we feel we should get or that we deserve. We may find ourselves comparing what we did for the individual and reflect on what we believe that they should do for us. I did _____ for you; therefore, you *should* do _____ for me. Entitlement Shovel Thoughts can look like this: "I did the wash and dried the clothes; therefore, you *should* fold them." Adjusting these thoughts to Ladder Thoughts (**E**valuate the Value) would look like this: "I want help with the household chores and would appreciate them helping. How can I express myself in a manner that will be productive and solution-focused?"

*Internalizing - My Fault Thinking.* When we internalize our expectations, we can also see it as blaming ourselves for problems, to include relationship problems. This is when we blame ourselves and think that bad things that happen are our fault. A "My Fault" type Shovel Thought looks something like: "It is my fault that my significant other and I can't get along. I *should* have done more. I led them to break up with me. I don't deserve happiness." We want to replace that with a Ladder Thought (Dissecting) like: "Relationships are a two-way street. If I did something that upset my significant other, then I would have liked to know exactly what it was so that I can change it in the future. I am not perfect, and neither are they."

The concern with "My Fault" thinking is that it can also lead to feelings of disappointment and sadness. The emotional toll can lead to individual and relationship struggles, resulting in an overall general decline in everyday functioning. "My Fault" thinking can also lead to repression and/or projection of responsibility.

*Summary of Expectations and Entitlements.* Expectations and entitlements often lead to internalized difficulties and potential conflict with others. We can find ourselves internalizing or externalizing expectations, or doing both. Learning to recognize and acknowledge our expectations and understand how these expectations and entitlements impact our own emotional well-being as well as our relationships will help reduce conflict and internal distress.

## Blaming and Responsibility

How often have you said to someone, "You made me angry." We may even find ourselves putting the responsibility of other emotions we experience on someone else. We use blaming statements when we think someone else is responsible for any problems we have. This often includes blaming others for our feelings or for "making us feel" a certain way or for "making us do" something. I often use experiential exercises in my therapy sessions, and I want to try one out with you. Please raise your right hand way above your head. Go ahead! No one has to see you raising your hand. Just raise your right hand way above your head. Is it there? If yes, then great! You let me take control over you, and you did exactly what I asked you to do. If you didn't, then great! You didn't let me take control over you. Just like you either let me control you, or you did not let me control you; I can't control you unless you relinquish control. People can't make you feel angry; you allow them to make you feel angry by thinking a certain way. No one can make you think, feel or do anything unless you give them power over you. One perspective on this is based on what Mahatma Gandhi said: "*Nobody can hurt me without my permission.*" This is often not easy given how we are conditioned to externalize responsibility. I often hear people state that "the teacher failed me" or "the cop gave me a ticket." However, often, the reality is that the individual may not have studied enough or that they were speeding. Our actions are frequently responsible for the consequences we experience.

I do acknowledge that life is not fair. I also can relate to having an adverse reaction when someone would tell me that life is not fair. However, at the end of the day, it usually isn't. I ultimately only have control over myself and changing *myself* versus *others*. I also really like Mahatma Gandhi's stand on this concept when he said: "*You can't change how people treat you or what they say about you. All you can do is change how you react to it.*" Part of this process is adjusting our thinking so that we can control our emotional reaction and then our behavioral reactions. Putting ourselves at risk of getting into a bad place (emotionally, behaviorally and/or due to consequences of our behaviors) will not help us in life.

When we use blaming statements, we usually try to come up with reasons why it is acceptable to forget something or mess something up or for getting back at someone. I find that people often carry around these resentments with them. I often use the metaphor of the resentments being like monkey poop that is put into a resentment container, waiting for the time when they can use it against the other person. When someone does something that you consider wrong or bad, an invisible piece of monkey poop is waiting on the floor, which you pick up and put into your monkey poop container with that person's name on it. You walk around with your monkey poop container until a situation arises or when you need justification for your behavior. To highlight this, consider the following: you come home, and you've forgotten to pick up your partner's dry cleaning. You see your partner and start thinking, "They are going to be upset with me." Then you prepare a counterattack by digging into your monkey poop container and preparing your comeback for when they make a comment regarding not picking up the dry cleaning. Your partner asks about the dry cleaning, and you say that you did not have a chance to pick it up. Your partner then expresses how they were depending on you to get their dry cleaning. You then dig into your container and throw a piece of that monkey poop at that person by saying:

"Well, if you would have _____, then maybe I would have picked up your dry cleaning."

Other ways in which blaming can be depicted include statements like: "I did _____ because you did _____." When we do this, we end up with monkey poop up to our necks and that relationship smelling like the poop.

Let's evaluate the scenario further. You come home and have forgotten to pick up your partner's dry cleaning and think, "They are going to be upset with me." Then they see you and negatively assume (although they assumed correctly) that you forgot to pick up the dry cleaning and confront you with it. Your Shovel Thought now builds to, "Well, she forgot to call in my medication refill. So what? What if I forgot to pick up her dry cleaning?" You then act on this Shovel Thought and say, "Maybe if you would have called in my medication refill, I would have remembered to pick up your dry cleaning." From here, you and your partner start throwing monkey poop at each other. Your partner may say, "If you would have left me a note, then I would have remembered to call in your medication refill." Again, we see the partner in this scenario blame the other person (you), placing the neglected medication refill call on you since you did not leave a note. So, how would one change this situation to result in a healthier outcome?

The first step in adjusting the Blaming and Responsibility Shovel Thoughts is to recognize our role in the process. This involves being aware of our emotional state and then identifying a Ladder Thought that would help adjust the process. Exploring the scenario and Shovel Thoughts in the previous paragraph helps provide context for Ladder Thoughts (**D**issecting and **E**valuate the Value) to help. A Ladder Thought may look like this: "They were counting on me to pick up their dry cleaning, and I forgot. It is my responsibility as I told them that I would do so. Focusing on what they may have forgotten in the past does not give me a pass. The best thing to do is apologize and see if I can make this up to them by picking up their dry cleaning as soon as possible. Otherwise, I will exhaust a lot of my emotional and physical energy into an argument that will benefit no one." As we can see, these Ladder Thoughts are often internal monologues that we can construct to help us climb over the barriers in our lives.

*Challenges of Not Allowing the Words or Actions of Others to Impact Us*

The concept of not allowing the words or actions of others to impact us emotionally can be very difficult. We are social creatures, and we do often care what others may say about us or to us. However, at the end of the day, they do not have power over us, and, with lots of practice, we can work on not allowing the words of others to negatively impact us.

There are some limitations, of course, when it comes to the kind of relationship you are in with the individual who says something hurtful. If the individual is a long-term romantic partner, spouse, etc., then their words may have a different meaning due to the significance of that relationship. The same can be said for parents, friends and others whom we may be more emotionally vulnerable with. In such cases, learning boundaries to help acknowledge the importance of the relationship while limiting their impact on us may be important if the relationship causes problems or starts to become toxic. These boundaries may include limiting our exposure to the individual, seeking relationship counseling or terminating the relationship. Ultimately, we have a choice to make as to whom we will have in our lives and to what degree we will allow them to impact us. I really appreciate Mahatma Gandhi's words when he said, "*I will not let anyone walk through my mind with their dirty feet.*" Gandhi's quote does highlight the importance of valuing ourselves enough to set limits and boundaries with others.

*Summary of Blaming and Responsibility*

Ladder Thoughts that focus on solutions and working together are often effective when challenging Blaming and Responsibility Shovel Thoughts. It is important to focus on taking responsibility for your thoughts, feelings and behaviors. Consider Mahatma Gandhi's thoughts on revenge: *"An eye for an eye makes the whole world blind."* Sometimes people purposely do things to get back at others. Gandhi's adage on revenge ("An eye for an eye...") shines a spotlight on the negative impact revenge has on relationships and the chaos it can cause. So, if a partner in a relationship thinks, "I'm not going to pick up her dry cleaning. She didn't call in my medication refill. Maybe next time I ask her to do something, she will remember," then revenge is present. This kind of thought may generate angry and vengeful feelings that result in similar behaviors. The resulting interpersonal interaction does not usually do anything but cause more chaos within relationships.

## Worst-Case Scenarios

Worst-Case Scenarios come in the form of Worst-Case Shovel Thoughts. They contribute to us feeling anxious, nervous, or worried. Worst-Case Scenarios can also be associated with hopelessness, helplessness, sadness, and anger. As simple as it sounds, these Worst-Case Shovel Thoughts focus on the worst-case outcomes and are problem-focused, not solution-focused. Some Worst-Case Shovel Thoughts can include thoughts like, "I am going to lose my job," "My partner and I are going to get a divorce," "They are going to find someone else and leave me," or "My daughter will fall and break her neck if I'm not there to protect her." Although some of these Worst-Case Shovel Thoughts may be possible, focusing on them will only lead to relationship and internal struggles while not necessarily preventing bad things from happening. Ask yourself these questions to help counteract Worst-Case Shovel Thoughts:

1) How is worrying about getting into an accident going to prevent potential future accidents?
2) How is worrying about a hurricane going to prevent a hurricane from coming or doing any damage?

I know some of you are thinking, "Well, I can be a more cautious driver." Yes, you can. Consider being a cautious driver and not an anxious one. Being cautious is reasonable as we can do our part to try to reduce the chance of accidents; however, driving around feeling anxious the entire time due to thinking that an accident will happen is not helpful or reasonable and can cause physical tension, potentially leading to worse driving.

Ladder Thoughts can be applied to focus on helpful factors to consider. One way to apply Ladder Thoughts is by combining **D**issecting Ladder Thoughts with **E**valuate the Value Ladder Thoughts: "I cannot prevent all car accidents from happening, and worrying about them will not help in any way. I can be a cautious and defensive driver while accepting that most things in life have some form of risk associated with the decision. Deciding to drive carries a risk of a possible accident. I can work on mitigating that risk by being a defensive driver. Let me focus my energy on defensive driving versus anxious driving."

*A note on anxiety, stress, worry and their relationship with worst-case thinking:* Stress, worry, and anxiety are often confused as the same thing. Anxiety is associated with something really bad happening in the future (American Psychiatric Association [APA], 2013). Stress, on the other hand, is the reaction to some stimuli or situation/event (APA, 2013). Now, there are situations or events that can cause distress, which is taxing on our systems, and we may not know how to manage such stress. On the other hand, there is eustress, which is healthy stress that can help us be more productive. Eustress can be a reaction to a situation or event, but the reaction pushes us to complete the task. Eustress has a purpose and can push us to complete tasks and get things done.

The second kind of stress is unproductive distress, which simply tortures us and is not helpful in any way. This unproductive stress can lead to a feeling of worry or anxiety. Now, if we don't act on the productive eustress, then we can inadvertently make it become unproductive distress with the same tormenting effect. The point is, if we can do something about it, then great, but, if not, consider not wasting time and energy and give ourselves a break from the agony within. Energy spent on stressful events or anxiety about dangers and misfortunes that we cannot control only tax our emotional and physical energy, resulting in a not so pleasant day, week, month, etc.

Additionally, living our lives based on *possibilities* versus *probabilities* can also lead to a lot of distress (e.g., anxiety, worry, stress, difficulties, etc.). If I live my life based on believing that I will win the lottery next week (a possibility), then I would buy a lot of things and quit work. However, quitting work and buying a bunch of things is not the healthiest choice to make since, although it is a possibility that I may win the lottery, it is not very probable. It is also possible that I may die in a car wreck on my way to work. If I lived based on possibilities, then I would potentially never leave my house. However, it is not probable that I will die in a car wreck on my way to work, so I leave the house and drive most days. The challenge is to remember to live our lives on *probabilities* versus *possibilities*.

One thing we can do to help alleviate some of the possible distress regarding possibilities in life is to take precautions. If my Worst-Case Shovel Thoughts include "I'm going to die in a car wreck, and my family will not be able to survive," then the only steps I can take to help myself is to be a cautious driver, acknowledge and accept that I cannot control how other people drive, and have enough life insurance that my family will be taken care of in case I do die. By putting my energy into what I can control versus fearing what I can't control, I can be more productive and focused on improving my life for the better.

The Serenity Prayer sums up this idea: *"God, grant me the serenity to accept the things I cannot change, the courage to change the things I can, and wisdom to know the difference"* (Reinhold Niebuhr). It really highlights the reality that we cannot control many things, and acceptance is probably the best solution. For those interested, the entire Serenity prayer can be found in Appendix A.

*Summary of Worst-Case Scenarios*

Worst-case Shovel Thoughts impact many individuals and relationships. Learn to recognize the themes and patterns that accompany these thoughts associated with worst-case scenarios. Jumping to conclusions with such devastating outcomes is likely to elicit unpleasant emotional reactions, such as anxiety and sadness. We can plan for potentially catastrophic situations, but we cannot necessarily prevent them from happening. The distress only worsens without plans and prepared responses to potentially tragic situations.

## This Always Happens (and/or) Here We Go Again

Have you ever had that "sixth sense" that something was about to happen? I'm not sure if I had a sixth sense, but I remember feeling like I knew in advance that things were going to happen. Later, I realized that it was all conditioning, classical conditioning to be exact. Remember that story about Dr. Pavlov and his dog? If not, I'll give you a quick refresher. Dr. Pavlov was a physiologist who was studying dogs. Whenever the door would open to the area containing a dog, a bell would ring. Normally, the researchers would be entering the area to bring the dogs food. Over time, Dr. Pavlov noticed that every time he opened the door (and the bell rang), the dogs salivated. They were expecting food even if he did not have food with him. This phenomenon is called classical conditioning as it showed that pairing some stimulus (e.g., a noise, a light, a picture, etc.) with some other experience (i.e., getting food) can result in an individual (or animal) reacting as if that experience were to occur solely when being exposed to the stimulus. One example may be whenever a child sees his dad come home with a bottle in a paper bag, he would automatically feel fear and run out of the house. When further explored, we realize that the child's father would often have a bottle of alcohol in the bag, and, when he got drunk, he would beat the child. Even if the father came home one day with a bottle of water in the bag, the child would still run as the conditioned stimulus (a bottle in a paper bag) would elicit the fear associated with being beaten, causing the child to run.

When I was a young boy, my father would bite his tongue right before he would spank us. I quickly made the association and mentioned it to my brothers and told them to run whenever Dad bit his tongue. Within a couple of days, we were able to test my hypothesis. My older brother was running around the house hitting me with a plastic sword. My father started to get annoyed, and he requested that we stop running around. Eventually, my father's patience had been exhausted. My father then bit his tongue, at which point I ran to my bedroom to hide under the bed. My brother did not heed my words and got his spanking early. Eventually, my father found me under my bed, and I got my spanking regardless. The point is that not everything in life is that simple to associate. There were times when my father bit his tongue, and he did not spank us. Unfortunately, we can get into an unhealthy habit of making these pre-determined situations and allow these future-seeing thoughts to influence us in an unhealthy way. [*Side note: My father was a wonderful man who loved us very much. We were never abused but did get the occasional spanking when we misbehaved.*]

When our thoughts include "Here we go again, I knew this was going to happen" or "This always happens," then we may start to get prepared for an event to occur. Sometimes, these events can be happy and/or exciting; however, many times, they tend to be not so happy events. These thoughts are often automatic and may be conditioned responses to past experiences and events. We start thinking that the event will happen again and again just because it happened once, twice or more often. We also allow the possibility of something happening to run our lives versus the probability of situations occurring. If I have ever gotten into a car accident, does that mean that I will always get into a car accident? No! However, if I choose to allow this kind of Shovel Thought to run my life, then I may find myself not ever driving due to the thought that I might get into another car accident.

Another sample of the "here we go again" or "this always happens" Shovel Thought is: "Last time I interviewed for a job, they never called me back. I might as well not even go." We want to replace this with a Ladder Thought (**D**issecting) like, "Just because I did not get the last job I interviewed for does not mean that I will not get this one. Even if I don't get this one, I can always go and apply other places and keep going until I get a job. Moreover, experience interviewing can prove beneficial in my job search."

We may also find ourselves thinking with these Shovel Thoughts when we start assuming that someone else is going to act a certain way. We see this happen most often with couples or in other interpersonal interactions. Your partner may say something that triggers the "here we go again" Shovel Thought, resulting in you preparing for battle by grabbing your "emotional" sword and shield and assuming your defensive mental stance. At this point, you are not paying attention to solutions or working together. Instead, you are just waiting to defend yourself and attack back. These "this always happens" or "here we go again" Shovel Thoughts are usually reactions to conditioning from past events. We see our significant other say or do something that we have associated with a not-so-positive event/interaction from the past, so we prepare ourselves for something negative to occur.

*Summary of "This always happens" or "Here we go again" Shovel Thoughts*

Trying to be prepared for potential negative outcomes and/or conflict can be almost as exhausting as the negative outcome and/or conflict itself. Working ourselves up and feeling anxious or angry will not prevent events from occurring. From a relational standpoint, the defensive stance with "sword and shield" in hand inadvertently invites conflict. When you find yourself internalizing these Shovel Thoughts, the thought itself is also being used to dig yourself into a hole of hopelessness, anxiety, frustration, or anger. Recognizing what triggers the conditioned thought and establishing Ladder Thoughts to keep you out of the hole will help you overcome the obstacle.

**All-or-Nothing Thinking**

Some people believe that you need to think big to make it big. At times, some people can get a little too extreme with their thoughts. A result of these extreme thoughts can be All-or-Nothing Thinking. All-or-Nothing thinking is often easily recognized when we say the words "Always" or "Never." Now, if these thoughts are positive thoughts (e.g., "My spouse is always nice to me" or "I always have a great time when I go out"), then such thinking may not necessarily be problematic but, when used negatively, they dig holes.

The steps to address All-or-Nothing Shovel Thoughts identified here are for times when such thoughts do cause some form of distress or conflict. An All-or-Nothing Shovel Thought may sound like, "You never trust what I say" or "He never calls when he is running late." Is it really *never*? He may not call *often* but does he really *never* call? Thinking in such extreme ways will lead to unhealthy feelings and possible unhealthy interactions. When we look at the Shovel Thought of "You always work late," ask yourself, "Is it really always?" If we think in these extreme ways, what kind of feelings are we going to have? Extreme feelings! If I think that you *always* do something or you *never* do something, then I am probably going to feel angry, sad, frustrated, hurt, or some other unpleasant emotion. Although, the "always" in All-or-Nothing can seem similar to the "This always happens," and, in some instances, it may feel the same. The concept is in the extreme thinking of All-or-Nothing thinking that is often paired with a *never*.

The All-or-Nothing thoughts can also manifest when we want things to always be one way or else. We think in all-or-nothing terms when we are usually extreme in our ideals. We often do not consider the middle ground and have feelings of frustration and anger if things are not conforming to our extreme thoughts. An All-or-Nothing Shovel Thought may look like: "You either support me in everything I say and do, or you do not love me." We want to replace the Shovel Thought with a Ladder Thought (**D**issecting) like, "I would like my partner to support me; however, they have a right to a different opinion and decision. The best thing is to try to compromise and meet in the middle so that we can both be happy." Another All-or-Nothing Shovel Thought is: "I'm never going to be happy." We can change this by using a Ladder Thought (**W**eighed and **E**valuate the Value) like, "I'm having a difficult time; however, I've been happy before in my life, and I can be happy again. There are no facts that support that I'm never going to be happy because I've been happy in the past. I can focus my energy on engaging in activities that have made me happy in the past. Trying different things can only be helpful. Focusing on these negative Shovel Thoughts will just expend my energy and bring me further down. I'm going to make changes in my life starting now." Additionally, the question of "How is thinking or feeling this way going to help me?" is important to explore in almost any distressful situation.

Lastly, remember the potential impact of self-fulfilling prophecies. We see self-fulfilling prophesies when someone repeatedly tells themselves something, and then, through the power of the mind-body connection, it happens. If I'm a wide receiver playing on a football team, and I start thinking, "I'm going to drop the ball. I'm going to drop the ball," then I am most likely going to drop the ball. However, if I say to myself, "I'm going to catch the ball. I'm going to catch the ball," then there is a greater chance that I will catch the ball. If I repeatedly think, "My partner is no good, and they can't be trusted," then I'm going to have a very hard time trusting them. I think Henry Ford said it best: "*Whether you think you can or think you can't, you're right.*"

*Summary of All-or-Nothing Shovel Thoughts*

Remember the hazards associated with extreme thinking when it comes to our emotions and interactions with others. With few exceptions (e.g., my partner always loves me…), the extreme "All-or-Nothing" thinking will cause difficulties and struggles. Consider the "what facts support this thought" (i.e., **W**eighed Ladder Thought process) step to help counteract these thoughts. When we look at the big picture, we tend to better recognize multiple factors to include the many positive aspects to relationships and experiences. Work on being appreciative and grateful for what you do have in life. Consider the role your family, friends, or loved ones play in your life. When doing this, remember the positive as it is rarely all negative. Consider the gratitude for that which you have versus resentment for what you may not have. Additionally, experiences with others (e.g., family members, co-workers, etc.) may be challenging at times, but defining the relationship by any struggles without exploring all the good times is just unfair.

**Body Messages**

The following Shovel Thoughts are often spurred on by some form of body sensation. This is when you have a physiological reaction (e.g., a pain or physical sensation somewhere), which triggers an unhealthy Shovel Thought, and then the not-so-pleasant emotional reaction. For example, "I feel my chest tightening up (physiological sensation). I must be having a panic attack (Shovel Thought). I'm feeling really anxious (emotion)." To counteract this Shovel Though, we can use Ladder Thoughts (**D**issecting and **E**valuate the Value) like, "I feel my chest tightening up, but it could be anything that is causing this sensation. It could be indigestion, fatigue or who knows what. I'm not having a panic attack because I'm not thinking anxious thoughts and therefore have not been feeling anxious. If I keep entertaining this idea that I'm having a panic attack, then I will have one, and that is not what I want. Instead, I'm going to do some slow breathing exercises to help relax my body."

At times, the body message may be due to being tired or having a lack of energy. I tend to think of part of Sir Isaac Newton's first law of physics: "*An object at rest stays at rest, and an object in motion will stay in motion…*" I find the same can be applied to humans. If we are lying in bed (body at rest), then automatically, for most people, our body may want to continue staying at rest. To get into an action stage, we almost have to push ourselves to get out of bed. However, we can always think our way into staying in bed (e.g., "I don't feel like getting up," "I'll go to the gym later" or "I'll take care of that later"). Ladder Thoughts (**Evaluate the Value**) to counteract these non-productive thoughts include focusing on the objective and repeatedly thinking that thought. Instead, one could think: "Get up, put clothes on, and go to the gym. Get up, put clothes on, and go to the gym" or "Get up and go take care of it now. Get up and go take care of it now." I remember when I was a young man, and my friends would call me to go hang out. I was so tired from graduate school, work, exercising, etc., that my first thought was, *I'm so tired, I'm going to have a horrible time there*. However, many times I would give in and go. Guess what? I never regretted going. I always had a great time and found energy in the interactions and positive experience with good friends. I have similar experiences in the morning when I wake up early to exercise. I do have some of those thoughts (e.g., "I'm too tired," "I should take a day off," etc.). However, I realized something years ago that helps me get up 99% of the time. I remind myself of the facts and the truth by saying to myself, *You have never regretted a workout. You always have more energy throughout the day when you exercise in the morning.*" These are ways of integrating positively focused All-or-Nothing Thinking.

Sometimes, these sensations can trigger other emotions. If I feel physically down or not feeling well, I may think, *I must be depressed.* These thoughts can often line up with the self-fulfilling prophecies addressed in the previous section of All-or-Nothing Shovel Thoughts. If you find yourself not feeling like you want to get moving, consider what Mahatma Gandhi said: "*Strength does not come from the physical capacity. It comes from an indomitable will.*" Please remember that your <u>will</u> and <u>commitment</u> are the keys to climbing out of the hole. Learning how to perform progressive muscle relaxation, breathing exercises, yoga, Tai Chi and/or using meditation applications are some behavioral methods to help with the mind-body connection to provide a calming and relaxing state if anxiety or stress-related physiological factors occur.

*Summary of Body Messages*

Being aware of our thoughts is part of the process of climbing over obstacles and not digging ourselves into emotional holes. Additionally, awareness of our physiological reaction in relation to our thoughts can also be extremely beneficial. Such awareness increases the likelihood that we can identify the Shovel Thoughts connected to the body message while developing helpful Ladder Thoughts to counteract them. Keep working on your awareness, write things down as they occur, and remember that emotions often tend to be a result of our thoughts.

## "And Then" Thinking (or) "What If" Thinking

And Then Shovel Thinking occurs when you think one bad or negative thing is going to happen, and then another, and then another all the way to a horrific outcome. It is like a negative domino effect of thoughts where one conjured negative outcome impacts/leads to the other. In other words, one Shovel Thought leads to another Shovel Thought, resulting in multiple scoops (digging with the shovel), making the emotional hole deeper and deeper. An example of an And Then Shovel Thought is, "I'm going to be late for work, and then my boss is going to give me 'the speech,' and then I'm going to get written up, which is going to negatively impact me when I go up for the promotion…" Instead, try replacing that Shovel Thought with Ladder Thoughts (**D**issecting and **E**valuate the Value) like, "Just because I'm late for work does not mean that all those other things are going to happen. Most times, no one is paying attention, and, even if they are, usually no one cares. Even if I do get written up, it does not define who I am as an employee and if it will interfere with a promotion. Getting upset about being late won't help me. I will put more effort into getting to work on time to reduce the chances of being late from happening in the future." As you can see from this scenario, one Shovel Thought can generate another Shovel Thought, and so on. The chain reaction of thoughts can build up and lead us to feel anxious, overwhelmed, sad, angry, or many other not-so-enjoyable emotions.

The And Then Shovel Thought pattern is like a gradual buildup to a semi worst-case thought. In the Worst-Case Shovel Thoughts, the anthill becomes the Himalaya Mountains. In the "and then" thinking, it is more like an anthill turning into a molehill, turning into a small hill, turning into a mountain, which *then* turns into the Rocky Mountains.

## "What If" Thinking

The What If Shovel Thought component can occur when we only look on the negative side of "what if" scenarios. As a metaphor, consider that there is a "what if" coin. On one side of the coin is the negative outcome that can occur; on the other side of the coin is the positive or neutral outcome. The negative side of the "what if" coin includes thoughts like, "What if my friend doesn't show up at the party"? "What if I don't know anyone there"? "What if people start to make fun of me"? The positive or neutral side of the "what if" coin includes the opposite: "What if my friend *does* show up at the party"? "What if I know everyone there"? "What if I have a great time?"

The What If Shovel Thoughts are like the And Then Shovel Thoughts with the exception that the former is more of a hypothetical view while the latter is a deterministic one. In other words, with the And Then Shovel Thought, one is thinking that it *will* happen. With the What If Shovel Thought, one is hypothetically thinking that it *may* happen. The "what if" coin concept can be used in many different situations. The important step to take when considering the "what if" coin is to look at all the facts. The Shovel Thought of "What if I fail the test"? is on the negative side of the coin. "What if I pass the test"? is on the positive side of the coin. When I ask myself, "How often has the coin toss landed on the negative side (i.e., What if I fail the test?)," I would likely answer, "At most, 10 times in my life." However, when I ask myself, "How often has the coin toss landed on the positive side (i.e., "What if I pass the test?") of the coin," I would likely answer, "Probably 500 times or more." When I do the math (10 divided by 510), I get an answer that indicates I have failed less than 2% of tests in my life. Most of the time, the positive side of the "what if" coin comes up. Given these numbers, I would realize that expending my energy on negative Shovel Thoughts about failing a test would not be in my best interest. Instead, I would realize that there is a significant probability (not just a possibility) that I will pass my test.

*Summary of "And Then" and "What If" Shovel Thoughts*

Some in the field have called these thought processes future-seeing or fortune telling. Our lives and futures are not necessarily spelled out for us, but we can change our thoughts and our lives to be better and healthier. Jumping to conclusions and working ourselves up into an emotionally charged state will tend to lead to emotional distress. To reduce the potential negative emotional impact of these types of thinking, we can remind ourselves of two things: 1) there are two sides to the "what if" coin; and 2) the potential negative domino effect of the and then" Shovel Thoughts are not guaranteed.

## Homework

Please complete the quiz in Appendix A to help you explore what types of Shovel Thoughts you tend to have. Continue to write down the thoughts and emotional reactions that come up in your life to better identify the Shovel Thoughts you typically experience most. Such information will help you continue to develop Ladder Thoughts for your pre-scripted journal. Remember that being prepared to counteract the Shovel Thoughts is very important and, at times, essential for this process to work.

## References

American Psychiatric Association. (2013). *Diagnostic and statistical manual of mental disorders* (5th ed.). https://doi.org/10.1176/appi.books.9780890425596

# CHAPTER 4

# BUILDING LADDER THOUGHTS

You have learned about the overall concept of CBT, common Feeling-Shovel Thought connections and more details about Shovel Thoughts. Now let's look at methods in which we can construct Ladder Thoughts to help a) climb over challenges (obstacles) that we experience; and b) climb out of emotional holes that we may have dug. Please remember that we cannot get rid of all Shovel Thoughts as they are often automatic. We want to learn to be aware of the Shovel Thoughts and build Ladder Thoughts to manage our emotions by counteracting the Shovel Thoughts. Consider that books and therapeutic approaches focused on anger are often titled "anger *management*" and not "anger *elimination*." The same can be said for "stress management." Instead of focusing on not having any Shovel Thoughts, focus your energy on developing healthy Ladder Thoughts to shift your emotional state and get to a better place.

Ladder Thoughts are the tools to help manage our emotions by not hyper-focusing or obsessing on the Shovel Thoughts. Additionally, Ladder Thoughts help us change our focus to climb out of emotional holes. Different approaches will be addressed; however, please consider that you can adjust any of these or develop a method that works for you. Keep an open mind and be cautious of Shovel Thoughts (e.g., "This won't work" or "This is too much work") that may enter your mind as you read through this chapter. Perhaps you can even develop some Ladder Thoughts to challenge such Shovel Thoughts.

## Review of The Ladder Thought Process

As you will recall from Chapter 1, there are three main categories of Ladder Thought development referred to as **D.E.W.** First, we build **D**issecting Ladder Thoughts that are directly related to the Shovel Thought and are strong enough to overcome them with the potential of a solution-focused perspective. Building these Dissecting Ladder Thoughts take practice, lots and lots of practice. The concept is to come up with something that directly challenges the Shovel Thought, piece-by-piece.

Second, the **E**valuate the Value Ladder Thought process involves exploring ways to try to quickly reframe your thinking to see if it will be emotionally beneficial to you. Simply thinking "How is thinking this way or feeling this way going to help anything?" is a quick way to get things started. We can focus on any emotional benefits of continuing to focus on Shovel Thoughts and what the eventual emotional cost (or emotional hole) will be. Then, we can decide whether we want to continue thinking or entertaining the Shovel Thoughts.

Third, we can work on the **W**eighed Ladder Thoughts by exploring any support for or against Shovel Thoughts, along with possible solutions. Remember, we are looking for facts, not opinions, that may or may not support Shovel Thoughts. You may find that some of the support you have thought of in the past has actually been opinions and not facts. If there is support for a Shovel Thought, then we focus on solutions to eventually change the belief or circumstance. In other words, what are you willing to do to change things for yourself? Chapter 5 will explain the Emotional Math process when the facts do support the Shovel Thought.

## Dissecting Ladder Thoughts

**D**issecting Ladder Thoughts focuses on breaking down components of Shovel Thoughts to help provide perspective and a solution-focused mentality. We take each section of the Shovel Thought and address it part-by-part. Often, we alter aspects of Expectation Shovel Thoughts to be desires instead. Changing the *should* to *I would like* is one way to shift the focus. Instead of thinking, "He should be here on time," we can think, "I would like him to be here on time; however, being upset about it is not going to make him magically appear. He will get here when he does, and I don't have to allow this to have a negative impact on my mood." As we can see, this process looks at dismantling the impact of the Shovel Thought so that we don't dig ourselves into an emotional hole.

Changing expectations to desires, recognizing that many needs are actually wants and separating out the extreme are all aspects of Dissecting Ladder Thoughts. The following section will provide some examples of Shovel Thoughts and ways in which to apply **D**issecting Ladder Thoughts to address them.

1) <u>What happened?</u> Somebody said something about me behind my back.

<u>How did I feel?</u> Betrayed

<u>Shovel Thought</u>: They shouldn't be spreading rumors. *(Expectation)*

<u>**D**issecting Ladder Thought</u>: I don't want people to spread rumors about me or to talk about me behind my back. Although this is a desire of mine, I can't stop people from doing so. However, I can control whom I discuss things with and whom I trust. I now know that it is not in my best interest to trust this person and to be careful with what I share with them. The fact is, I've probably said things about others behind their backs, and I want to start living and treating people as I want to be treated. Therefore, I'm going to work on not talking about others and accept that others may still do it to me. Being upset about this will only negatively impact me, so I'm going to focus on making my day the best day possible and not focus on things I cannot control.

2) <u>What happened?</u> Traffic due to people slowing down to look at an accident on the side of the road.

<u>How did I feel?</u> Frustrated

<u>Shovel Thought</u>: What is going on with these people? Don't they know how to drive? They should stop looking over to the side of the road and just let traffic flow versus slowing down to be nosy. What a bunch of idiots. *(Expectation)*

<u>**D**issecting Ladder Thought</u>: People are going to be people, and traffic

is traffic. Traffic is difficult enough as it is, and sitting in it while frustrated or angry is not going to help the traffic flow any faster. Let me focus my energy on something that will be as enjoyable as possible while I'm in traffic. I can be proactive and call to let my \_\_\_\_\_ (e.g., partner, work, etc.) know that I'm in traffic and may be late. I can listen to some good music or call someone to make the most of the situation.

3) <u>What happened?</u> Someone else got promoted, and you did not.

<u>How did I feel?</u> Disappointed or jealous

<u>Shovel Thought</u>: Kevin got the promotion. I should have gotten the promotion over him. This is not fair, and it's not right. *(Expectation)*

**D**<u>issecting Ladder Thought</u>: I really wanted that promotion and believe that I was not only qualified but deserving of the next step in my career. I do believe that I could do a better job than Kevin, but this is not Kevin's fault. He wants to move forward just as much as I do. For whatever reason, the powers that be felt he was a better candidate. I'm going to request a meeting with my supervisor to see what I can do to be considered top-of-the-list for a promotion next time one comes around. Focusing my energy on what I can do is probably better than staying disappointed about something I cannot change.

4) <u>What happened?</u> Your partner does not do the dishes when it is their turn to do so.

<u>How did I feel?</u> Frustrated

<u>Shovel Thought</u>: Don't want to do the dishes on your "dishes chore night." Fine! See how it feels to not have any clean clothes tomorrow because I don't want to do my laundry chore tonight. *(Expectation and Blaming)*

**D**<u>issecting Ladder Thought</u>: I would want my partner to do the dishes and to complete any assigned chore. Staying frustrated won't make the dishes clean themselves. Neither my partner nor I is perfect. I sometimes inadvertently forget to do something, and I am thankful when I get a friendly reminder or when someone offers to help me take care of my responsibilities. The best thing to do is to offer for us to help each other. We can do the dishes and the laundry together.

5) <u>What happened?</u> Your significant other breaks up with you.

<u>How did I feel?</u> Sad, lonely or defeated.

<u>Shovel Thought</u>: I'll never find someone who will want to be with me. *(Worst-Case)*

**D**issecting Ladder Thought: Relationships are difficult, and I do miss my partner. However, I've known people to be in other relationships, and I'll have an opportunity to find someone else. I'm being too extreme-thinking that I'll never find someone to be with me because that is not likely. The only way I won't be in another relationship is if I don't allow myself to be open to the idea of another relationship. It is in my best interest to grieve this loss and regroup, focus on myself, and get back out in the dating world again when I'm ready.

6) <u>What happened?</u> You were going on a second date with someone, and they stood you up.

<u>How did I feel?</u> Abandoned, sad, hurt, disappointed, or defeated.

<u>Shovel Thought</u>: Is there something wrong with me? This always happens. They stand me up after the first date and never call me. This is going to keep happening, and then I'm going to end up dating repeatedly with just being disappointed and hurt over and over again. Then I'm going to end up just working all my life without a lifelong companion. Ultimately, I'm going to die a lonely soul, and no one will attend my funeral because no one cares. *(This Always Happens/Here We Go Again)*

**D**issecting Ladder Thought: Let me think here. I've had long-term relationships in the past, and I know I can have another one. I've known people who were stood up before and who had to keep dating to find someone with whom they could build a relationship. Even if I struggle to find a suitable romantic relationship, I have friends and family members who love me and who will always be in my life. I know that they will be there for me now and at my funeral. If my date didn't want to see me again, then it is their loss, and I just need to get back out there and keep working on this.

7) <u>What happened?</u> Your kids want to have a friend stay overnight, but it is a work night for you. You say "no" due to not being able to supervise, and your kids say you never let me do anything.

<u>How did I feel?</u> Guilt.

<u>Shovel Thought</u>: It is my fault that my children are not happy. *(My Fault)*

<u>**D**issecting Ladder Thought</u>: Guilt implies responsibility for something that hurts or wrongs someone else. My children not having someone over does not hurt them, and it does not mean that I am wronging them. I do want my children to be happy and to have fun, and I can only do so much within reason to help them in their pursuit of happiness. Additionally, I have other responsibilities that need to be met for them to be happy and safe. Work is necessary, in my case, to have an income to support my family. Supervising minors is also part of my responsibility as a parent. There is nothing to be guilty of in this case because I'm doing what is necessary to provide for my family.

**Evaluate the Value Ladder Thoughts**

**E**valuate the Value Ladder Thoughts to identify what our emotional state of being would be if we continued to think in a certain manner. In other words, what good or what benefit will come out of thinking a certain way. If the answer is a negative result, negative emotional reaction or negative outcome of some type, then the focus would be on changing the thought process by continually re-examining and repeating the outcome. To put this further into perspective, I want to quote Lionel Robbins' definition of economics: "…the study of the use of scarce resources which have alternative uses" (as cited by Sowell, 2015, p. 2). My physical and emotional energy are scarce resources in my life. I only have so much of each, and, although I can push myself, I can still get physically and/or mentally exhausted. I don't want to focus my energy on thoughts that will drain me emotionally. Instead, I want to focus my energy on thoughts and activities that will result in positive experiences and gains.

One metaphor that demonstrates this is the concept of investments. Millions of people around the world, and in the United States in particular, pour money into investments in hopes of increased wealth and prosperity. If you have a 401(k), an Individual Retirement Account (IRA, Traditional or Roth) or a 403(b), then you have some understanding of investing your money for positive gains. However, imagine an investment strategy that only resulted in negative returns. Would you invest your money into a product, process, or account that only resulted in you losing money? Most people would not. We want to consider the same with our thought processes and our emotional energy. If we spend our emotional energy on a thought that provides no positive return but instead a negative return, then spending any more energy on those Shovel Thoughts would not be helpful.

Imagine that you start your day with 100 emotional dollars. Consider how many of those emotional dollars are needed for different responsibilities in your life. When you have a Shovel Thought, imagine that you are putting some or all of those emotional dollars into the Shovel Thought account. What will happen to those emotional dollars? Will you get a positive return or experience for investing your emotional dollars on Shovel Thoughts? More likely than not, you will lose all of those emotional dollars. Additionally, there is a possibility that you will inadvertently put more emotional dollars, if any are left, into that Shovel Thought account, resulting in a greater loss if you continue to dwell and obsess on the Shovel Thoughts.

Start by asking yourself, "Will thinking this way get me a positive emotional return or a negative emotional return"? Additionally, remember to consider the other "returns" in your life. What will the physical, economic, social, relational, etc., be if you continue to think with Shovel Thoughts versus Ladder Thoughts?

The following scenarios will provide **E**valuate the Value Ladder Thoughts to address different Shovel Thoughts.

1) <u>What happened?</u> My child goes to a friend's house for a pool party.

<u>How did I feel?</u> Worried, anxious, or fearful.

<u>Shovel Thought</u>: What if they drown? *(Worst-Case)*

<u>**E**valuate the Value Ladder Thought</u>: My child has taken swim lessons, and there will be other adults there to supervise the children. Sitting

here worrying about my child drowning is not going to help them nor is it going to help me. Putting my energy into worrying about this will only put me into a negative emotional hole. I've done everything reasonable to reduce the chances of something bad happening. My child knows how to swim. I know the parents there and trust them. Even if something were to happen to my child, worrying about it would not help them. I'm going to spend my time and energy focusing on something that I can enjoy and allow my child to enjoy their time.

2) <u>What happened?</u> My child is going on a field trip and taking a school-chartered bus.

<u>How did I feel?</u> Worried, anxious, or fearful.

<u>Shovel Thought</u>: What if the bus gets into an accident and my child gets hurt or dies? *(Worst-Case)*

<u>Evaluate the Value Ladder Thought</u>: I can't control what happens in life, and worrying about this is just going to put me in a bad place. The drivers of these buses are professionals, and they are held accountable. If I stop my child from doing anything due to the possibility of any danger, then my child will live a sheltered and potentially unhappy life. I don't want to impede my child's happiness or their experiences because of any possible danger that can happen in life. I'm going to do something for me today and focus my energy on positive experiences.

3) <u>What happened?</u> My partner has not yet come home. I call, and it goes straight to voice mail.

<u>How did I feel?</u> Worried or anxious.

<u>Shovel Thought</u>: What if something happened to him? Did he get in a car accident and get hurt? *(Worst-Case)*

<u>Evaluate the Value Ladder Thought</u>: He is 30 minutes late, and the traffic can get pretty backed up at times. Perhaps the phone ran out of battery life, or he forgot to turn it on. Regardless, worrying about something happening will not help him or me in any way. Channeling this energy into worrying will just make me feel horrible until they make it home. I'm going to focus my energy on things that will be helpful right now and just leave a message and send a follow-up text.

4) <u>What happened?</u> I got notified today that I'm being laid off from my job.

<u>How did I feel?</u> Worried.

<u>Shovel Thought</u>: What am I going to do now? How will I pay the bills? Now I must go find a job in such a difficult work environment. I may not find a job for several months, and I'm not going to be able to afford the house, groceries, or my car. Then I'm going to lose everything and have to move back in with my parents. Then I'm just going to be stuck there for the rest of my life and not be happy. *(And Then Thinking)*

<u>Evaluate the Value Ladder Thought</u>: Getting upset about this and being anxious about the future will not help me find a job. I'll benefit more from focusing my energy on getting my resume together, asking people about job opportunities, searching the job sites and reducing my expenses. I can be happy with any job while I keep looking as long as it helps provide for my needs. I'll meet with Human Resources to see if there is a severance package with the layoff and plan on making the best I can with what I have.

5) <u>What happened?</u> My friends had a party and they forgot to invite me.

<u>How did I feel?</u> Disappointed.

<u>Shovel Thought</u>: Why would they do this to me? Do I mean that little to them? They should have thought about me. *(Expectation)*

<u>Evaluate the Value Ladder Thought</u>: Missing one party and being forgot about in one situation does not mean that I'm not important to them. I've forgotten things in my life, and no one (and no group) is perfect. The party is over, and focusing my energy on feeling disappointed isn't going to help anyone. I'm going to focus on working with my friends to figure out a way we can always include each other so that this does not happen to me or any of them in the future.

6) <u>What happened?</u> I've been working overtime for two weeks, and my check did not reflect the additional pay.

<u>How did I feel?</u> Angry.

<u>Shovel Thought</u>: They should have paid me for the time I've worked. I can't believe that they are trying to rob me out of my hard-earned money. *(Expectation)*

<u>E</u>valuate the Value Ladder Thought: Mistakes happen in life, and putting my energy into being upset and angry won't make my money magically appear. I'm only going to get more upset and angrier if I keep focusing on what I think they *should* have done. It would be in my best interest to stay calm, go through the appropriate channels to request that they review my work hours and pay me for the additional overtime pay.

7) <u>What happened?</u> My hometown team lost the game.

<u>How did I feel?</u> Sad or defeated.

<u>Shovel Thought</u>: We will never get to the championships. *(All-or-Nothing)*

<u>E</u>valuate the Value Ladder Thought: Thinking we will never get to the championships is somewhat extreme. I want the team to win and to move forward; however, being sad about it is not going to help anyone, in particular not the team or myself. I'm sure I will get more benefit from focusing on things I enjoy rather than the negative aspects of life. I'm going to focus my energy on something that will be helpful.

8) <u>What happened?</u> Going through a divorce.

<u>How did I feel?</u> Guilty.

<u>Shovel Thought</u>: I should have worked harder at it so that my children won't suffer. *(My Fault- Internalized Expectation)*

<u>E</u>valuate the Value Ladder Thought: I can't change the past, and, although I don't like how difficult this has been on us, I realize that I could not control my spouse. We both share responsibility for the divorce, and focusing my energy on beating myself up will result in feelings of guilt and sadness. This has been hard enough, and I don't want to waste my physical or emotional energy focusing on things I cannot

control as the divorce is in process. I will focus my energy on spending time with my children so that they know they are loved. Moving forward, I'm going to focus on changing what I can with my children versus beating myself up about the past.

**Weighed Ladder Thoughts**

**W**eighed Ladder Thoughts weigh the facts that support or do not support the Shovel Thoughts. In other words, it's best to try to take an objective look (specific facts) at the Shovel Thought versus solely looking at the opinions or perceptions (subjective look). We just want to sit and think about how factual the thinking is instead of simply accepting it as fact. Please remember that opinions are not facts. They are often preferences or views, which may have no actual basis in fact. Additionally, many of us have heard the comment about opinions: *opinions are like armpits - everyone has two, and they usually stink.*

If we determine that the Shovel Thought does have enough support to be considered, then we shift the Ladder Thought process to the **E**valuate the Value Ladder Thought approach to determine what we can better spend our energy on to make a difference for the positive and overcome the obstacle. Another option will be covered in Chapter 5 (Emotional Math). The following scenarios will demonstrate Shovel Thoughts and ways in which to apply **W**eighed Ladder Thoughts to address them.

*Supporting Facts*

The **W**eighed Ladder Thought process includes exploring any facts that support the thought and any facts that do not.

1) <u>What happened?</u> You come home, and the house is a mess. Your partner has been home all day alone.

<u>How did I feel?</u> Angry.

<u>Shovel Thought</u>: If they respected me, then they would not embarrass me by leaving the house messy. They would respect me by cleaning the house more often. *(All-or-Nothing)*

<u>**W**eighed Ladder Thought</u>: What support do I have for the thought

that they do not respect me? How does someone not cleaning the house equate to disrespect? I wonder in what ways they do respect me. I'm going to list the ways in which I feel respect from my partner and express my preference for more help with having the house cleaned. I will explore how we can work together so that we can both be happier with the duties and responsibilities of the house.

2) <u>What happened?</u> You are going to the mall to buy something for a friend's birthday.

<u>How did I feel?</u> Worried.

<u>Shovel Thought</u>: Everyone's going to be looking at me and judging me negatively. *(Worst-Case)*

**W**<u>eighed Ladder Thought</u>: I don't know if people are going to look at me (this is not a 100% fact). Even if they do look at me, I don't have any support that they are going to judge me negatively. In fact, most people are too busy spending time with other people or focused on what they have to buy. Even if they were to judge me, then it would say more about them then me. I'm going to make sure I don't judge people negatively since it is what I can do to make myself better and the world a better place.

3) <u>What happened?</u> Your significant other breaks up with you.

<u>How did I feel?</u> Sad.

<u>Shovel Thought</u>: No one will ever love me. *(Worst Case and All-or-Nothing)*

**W**<u>eighed Ladder Thought</u>: Just because one person does not want to be with me does not mean that no one will ever love me. The reality is that my significant other had to have positive feelings toward me, or we would not have been in a relationship in the first place. Relationships come and go, and, at times, that also means that loving feelings come and go. There is no support for the thought that "no one will ever love me." In fact, many people do love me and have loved me.

4) <u>What happened?</u> Applied for multiple jobs, and none of them responded.

How did I feel? Disappointed.

Shovel Thought: I'm not good enough. No one will ever hire me. *(Worst-Case and All-or-Nothing)*

Weighed Ladder Thought: Not getting a job does not mean I'm not good enough. What facts would support me not being good enough? I realize that sometimes jobs go to friends or family members. Also, just because someone may be more qualified for a job does not mean that I'm not good enough for that job. What facts support that I am good enough? I met the educational and experience requirements for the job; therefore, I'm good enough for the job. My energy is better spent focusing on what I can do now to be an even better candidate for future job openings.

5) What happened? My boss directed me to do something that I know will not work. However, my boss will not hear me out and just redirects me to do what they said.

How did I feel? Frustrated.

Shovel Thought: This is a waste of my time. Why am I doing this? Why do this when it is a waste of my time? *(Expectation)*

Weighed Ladder Thought: What facts are there that this is a waste of my time? When I think about this, I'm getting paid to do what my boss directs me to do. My time is reimbursed regardless of the outcome. Therefore, there is no real support that this is a waste of my time because I'm getting paid for my time.

6) What happened? I took my certification exam for the second time and failed again.

How did I feel? Defeated.

Shovel Thought: I'm not smart enough or capable enough of passing this. *(Worst-case)*

Weighed Ladder Thought: What facts are there that support the thought that I'm not smart enough? I completed the educational component and passed all of the requirements. I have passed over 40 courses and hundreds of exams to get to this point. I've only failed this twice. I've passed much more than I have failed, which means the facts actually support that I *am* smart enough. Giving up is not going to help me in this situation. I realize it took Thomas Edison over 5,000 tries to invent the light bulb. It was not a question of him being smart enough; it was a question of him figuring it out. I would benefit more from focusing on how to pass. What can I do differently to study in a manner to help me be successful at passing this test?

7) <u>What happened?</u> Your child agreed to give a neglected pet away. When the day came to deliver the pet to the new owners, your child throws a tantrum saying that they changed their mind.

<u>How did I feel?</u> Guilty.

<u>Shovel Thought</u>: It's my fault that my child is suffering. I should have known that she would be upset and should have done something else to prevent it from happening. (*My Fault - Internalized Expectation*)

<u>**W**eighed Ladder Thought</u>: What facts are there that support the notion that this is my fault? My child, whether I like it or not, neglected the pet. What is a fact is that children can be temperamental, and they do change their minds. What is *not* a fact is that I am a mind reader and that I *should* know when and how things will happen. This is what is best for the pet, for my child and for myself. Life lessons can sometimes be painful; that is just part of life.

## Homework

Remember, the only way to get better at something is to practice it repeatedly. Whenever you have an experience and resulting unpleasant emotional reaction, grab your journal and go through the Ladder Thought building process. Write everything out and reflect on how you can adjust your thought patterns. I appreciate what Patrick Rothfuss said: *"Practice makes the master."* Therefore, if I want to become the master of my emotional life, it will include practicing ways to better manage my emotional reactions.

## References

Sowell, T. (2015). *Basic economics: A common sense guide to the economy* (5th ed.). Basic Books.

# CHAPTER 5

# EMOTIONAL MATH

One Ladder Thought approach can include the practice of some Emotional Math. Emotional Math is the process of writing down the equations we have in our mind that often reinforce our emotional state. These equations are more likely to be associated with beliefs we have about ourselves versus a thought by itself (refer to Chapter 1 for a brief review). Let's say Danny believed that no one would ever love him. Then Danny may have an equation in his mind that resembled the following:

Danny = unlovable

We would use Emotional Math to evaluate the equation and explore if it is an accurate equation. To do this, we may look at what unlovable means. In essence, unlovable means that no one would ever love the person. In this case, if there is anyone in Danny's life who has ever loved him, then this equation would not be accurate. Therefore, we would ask Danny to rewrite his equation to:

Danny = someone who has been loved

The reality for many of us is that these extreme equations and ways of thinking often come into our minds; however, they are not usually accurate. Another way to look at it would be if Danny were hard on himself whenever he did not score a perfect 100% on a test or if he did not get a 5 (exceeds expectations) on his work evaluation. Here, we could see Danny likely having an equation that stated:

Danny = *must* be perfect all the time

Expecting to be perfect is a lot of pressure that is truly unfair as no one is perfect. We can find ourselves using a lot of self-blaming Shovel Thoughts that only bring us down, resulting in us emotionally beating ourselves up. This often happens when we impose such a high expectation. As Salvador Dali said, *"Have no fear of perfection - you'll never reach it."* Instead of focusing on perfection, I encourage focusing on mastery, excelling at what one does and focusing on improvements. Therefore, a **W**eighed Ladder Thought would look like: "No one is perfect, so expecting that of myself will only lead to me emotionally torturing myself. This equation is unfair and unreasonable. No one would ever have support for such a thought, and it is unfair to put this much pressure on myself."

We can also break down the equation further and work through the process. Let's start with the first equation and try to find what is at the core:

1) Danny = *Must* be perfect all the time
    a. We then move the right side of the equation over to the left (see step 2) by "subtracting" it from both sides. Therefore, the right side would be blank, and the left side would have the opposite (we change the "having" to "not being")

2) Danny *not being perfect* all the time = ?
    a. Here, we try to figure out what is behind this urge to be perfect all the time by determining what it would mean if Danny were not perfect all the time.

3) Danny *not being perfect* all the time = Danny *not being deserving of love*

4) If Danny *is not deserving of love* = Danny *will live his life alone*

5) Danny *being alone* = *experiencing emotional agony*

Now, we can see that at the core of the pressure Danny puts on himself is a fear of being alone as he associates being alone with experiencing emotional agony. In this case, what would be the best use of Danny's energy? Would he be better served by trying to be perfect all the time so that he will believe that he is deserving of love, have someone be with him and avoid experiencing emotional agony? Or, would he be better served by working on accepting and/or learning: a) how to not experience emotional agony when alone, embracing aloneness and focusing his energy on things that help him cope with being alone? b) that love is something we all deserve but it takes compromise, patience, sacrifice, and work? and c) that fear will often lead to control and control is not compromising, sacrificing, or patient, which will likely result with me being alone? In this case, the underlying emotion that is pushing the perfection concept is fear, as in: I fear experiencing emotional agony so I must be deserving of love, and to deserve love I must be perfect.

*A note for parents:* Parents often inadvertently put a lot of pressure on their children. Many of us see that our children are capable of getting an A on tests or at the end of the semester or nine weeks in some classes. At times, our children will get mainly As and Bs in all their classes. We then impose this pressure onto our children when they don't perform at the same level every time. I dare to say that this is unfair to our children. Do we perform at 100% capacity 100% of the time with our work? Do we perform at 100% capacity 100% of the time as parents? Do we perform at 100% capacity 100% of the time in other relationships and other areas of life? I can honestly say that I don't. Therefore, it would be unfair to impose such high-level expectations on my children. I want to free them and myself of such unhealthy pressure. However, I can encourage and support my children when they are not performing at 100% capacity.

### *What do we do if we find that a significant portion of the equation is correct?*

If an equation is correct, then we focus on what we can do to change the equation. If Danny's belief is accurate (i.e., Danny = unlovable), then we would take the following steps:

First, we want to make sure that we clarify how the equation is correct and remove any All-or-Nothing concepts. Therefore, we would explore the following equation change to:

Danny = sometimes unlovable

If Danny does or doesn't do certain things that really do make it difficult for him to be lovable, then we would look for ways to adjust the equation. To adjust our Emotional Math (just like in regular math), we would want to add, subtract, multiply, etc. something. In this case, we may look at adding behaviors and/or attitudes to the equation:

> What can we add to Danny (i.e., what can Danny do or how can Danny be) for him to be more lovable? One way to conceptualize this is:

> Danny + being friendlier and nicer to people = being more lovable

Please remember that we reap greater benefits from focusing our cognitive (thoughts), physical and emotional energy into improving situations versus beating ourselves up. In other words, using Emotional Math and Ladder Thoughts to help us overcome emotional and interpersonal barriers is a much better use of our energy compared to using that energy to dig ourselves into deeper emotional holes.

**Homework**

Review your journal and identify any possible beliefs versus thoughts. Do you see any patterns or themes regarding thoughts that may have an underlying belief? Consider how you can also use Emotional Math to challenge other Shovel Thoughts to help you focus your energy on producing a more realistic and positively focused state of mind. Work through your beliefs and thoughts using Emotional Math and Ladder Thoughts to alter them to be more productive and positive.

# CHAPTER 6

# FORGIVENESS

When we don't forgive someone, it may mean that we are wallowing in resentment or anger. Throughout my years as a clinician, I have found that grudges and anger toward others can lead to a deep emotional hole. Shovel Thoughts associated with revenge, anger, grudges, and wanting some sense of justice can really dig big and deep emotional holes. Forgiveness of self and forgiving others is an essential part of living a healthy and happy life. The weight of resentment and anger that we are holding against someone else still impacts us negatively. Learning to let go of past hurts and mistakes is vital to climbing out of emotional holes and moving forward in life.

One perspective that highlights the hazards of not forgiving comes from a quote of Marianne Williamson, who said, *"Unforgiveness is like drinking poison yourself and waiting for the other person to die."* I want to acknowledge the late Dr. George Hay for introducing me to that quote. This quote helps emphasize the value of building Ladder Thoughts and freeing ourselves from the poison we consume when we don't forgive. Lewis B. Smedes presented this idea in another way: *"To forgive is to set a prisoner free and discover that the prisoner was you."* These concepts help highlight how we can get trapped in a deep emotional hole of unforgiveness. Often, the only way out of the unforgiveness emotional hole is to build forgiveness-oriented Ladder Thoughts. Know that you don't ever have to tell the other person that you forgive them. Forgiving them in your heart and not holding it against them is the key. Also remember that forgiving them doesn't mean that you have to allow yourself to get emotionally or physically close to them. You can forgive without reconciling with someone. In other words, you can forgive someone in your heart for what they did and at the same time maintain boundaries to keep yourself physically and emotionally safe from them. Forgiveness does not equal making up; however, if you do want to reconcile, then forgiveness is often necessary. I find it difficult to allow myself to be emotionally vulnerable with someone when I have not forgiven them.

## Forgiveness of Self

At times, we can be our own worst critic, and such internal criticism can result in a pattern of internal discontent. There may be just as much value in forgiving *oneself* as there is in forgiving *others*. We often put unrealistic demands or expectations upon ourselves, which may be difficult to reach. We may expect perfectionism from ourselves thinking that we are struggling to be in a better place only to find ourselves in a deep emotional hole. Mahatma Gandhi said: *"Freedom is not worth having if it does not include the freedom to make mistakes."* Such wise words, along with Salvador Dali's quote from the previous chapter, *"Have no fear of perfection - you'll never reach it,"* are helpful in highlighting the importance of accepting our mistakes. By forgiving ourselves, we allow ourselves the freedom to be human and make mistakes. Forgiveness of self is one way to be gentle and loving with ourselves. We can work on not repeating mistakes; however, forgiving ourselves is an important part to self-healing.

Self-forgiveness is often easier when we can have self-compassion. Consider the situation, event, or action that you are holding against yourself. Now, imagine your child (or if you don't have children, imagine someone you care about) telling you that they are emotionally beating themselves up for what they did and can't seem to forgive themselves. What would you tell your child or other person you care about? Would you tell them to keep on punishing themselves? Would you encourage them to forgive themselves? I'm going to venture a guess and say that you would tell them to forgive themselves. Self-compassion is treating ourselves with the same love and compassion as we do those we care about. By integrating self-compassion, forgiveness of self can be much easier.

## Steps to Forgiveness

Forgiveness is easier said than done. Frank Friedman emphasized that forgiveness is not a one-time event but instead first a decision and then a process. For example: someone hits me with a baseball bat. When I don't forgive, I consistently emotionally hold the baseball bat event against the other person. Every time I think of the baseball bat event, I become angry and resentful. Therefore, the steps to forgiveness are as follows (keep in mind that a journal will be required):

1) Write down what it is (i.e., the event or situation) that you are holding against yourself or others.
2) Decide to forgive the other person or yourself. In other words, a decision not to hold it against yourself or others.
3) Next to the event or situation, write today's date (or whatever day it is that you decide to forgive) and write that you have decided to forgive.
4) If you get angry or resentful or down on yourself when you think about the event or situation, then go to your journal and remind yourself that you have forgiven yourself or the other person(s).
5) Repeat steps 1 through 4 for every event or situation that you are harboring anger or resentment about.
6) Remember to incorporate Ladder Thoughts (**E**valuate the **V**alue) to help with the process.

*Forgiveness example:*

1) The event: You find out that your fiancé broke up with you because she was romantically involved with someone else.
2) I'm going to forgive her for the betrayal of my trust and for the resulting pain that I have experienced.
3) On November 4, 2005, I have decided to forgive my ex-fiancé for cheating on me. I am not going to hold this against her anymore.
4) If the thought of the betrayal and any remaining pain comes up, I go back to my journal and remind myself that I have already decided to forgive her.
5) I will apply the **E**valuate the **V**alue Ladder Thought to explore what value I am getting from holding on to the

betrayal. Is this helping me or helping anything? Am I hurting myself emotionally for nothing? What would be a better way to spend my emotional energy?

I respect that this process may not be easy, and, at times, one may not be ready to forgive. This is something that we will all have to make a decision about. Remember the **E**valuate the Value Ladder Thought process and explore what value you're getting from holding on to the resentment, anger, or hurt. Is it in your best interest to forgive and free yourself of the unpleasant emotions, or is it a better for you to hold on to those emotions?

**Homework**

Explore the areas of your life that would benefit from forgiveness. What are you holding against yourself? What have you been holding against others? If you feel or decide that you are ready for forgiveness, then go through the steps and work through the process of forgiveness. Remember the value of writing these steps out and getting them out of your mind and into action.

# CHAPTER 7

# PERSONAL ADJUSTMENTS AND SUPPLEMENTAL METAPHORS

I enjoy exploring different analogies and metaphors to use with clients and students. The Ladders and Shovel concept came to me one time when working with a client, and I could see the benefits of visualization when conceptualizing emotions and change. We are all unique, and a different approach, concept, or presentation of the information may help increase the chances that more people will be able to implement change. Additionally, consider whatever concept, analogy, metaphor, etc., that would help you better apply thought-changing procedures to improve your emotional state.

**Dynamite Stick**

Imagine a stick of dynamite. When a situation occurs (i.e., the "what happened"), it is like a lighter being struck and the potential of the dynamite fuse getting lit. A Shovel Thought would represent the lighting of the fuse. If the fuse is not cut off or extinguished, then the dynamite stick may end up exploding (emotional explosion). Now, the explosion may not be an anger explosion; it could be an explosion of anxiety, sadness or some other feeling. By being aware of all facets of this process, it increases the possibility of catching the fuse early to cut it off or extinguishing it from continuing to burn. Sometimes, your fuse burns out before an explosion, but the fuse is automatically shorter. When fuses are short, they present a risk for quick emotional outbursts due to low thresholds or tolerance. Also consider how your interpersonal interactions while emotionally charged (i.e., with a lit fuse) could increase the chances of interpersonal discord.

We can, however, work on lengthening our fuse back to its original threshold by processing our thoughts and emotions through the written exercises described earlier in this book.

## House on Fire

Visualizing your mind as a house is another way to conceptualize the importance of being aware of our thoughts and changing them before they cause too much damage. A Shovel Thought is like a small flame in one of the rooms in your house. Adding additional Shovel Thoughts, or entertaining any Shovel Thought for more than a couple of minutes, will fuel the fire, and the fire will spread. Before you know it, the whole room will be on fire. Then the fire can spread to the rest of the house. It would be much easier to extinguish that small flame (Shovel Thought) with an extinguisher (Ladder Thought) compared to trying to put out the fire of an entire room or house. Working on identifying these flames (Shovel Thoughts) early will help you extinguish (with Ladder Thoughts) the fires and maintain a less hazardous and conflict-driven relationship. Additionally, you could change the terms of the types of thoughts if you find this metaphor more helpful. You can call the disruptive thoughts Fire Thoughts (instead of Shovel Thoughts) and the helpful thoughts Extinguisher Thoughts (instead of Ladder Thoughts).

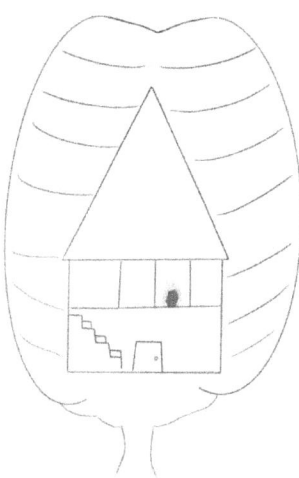

## Computer Programmer

Our experiences throughout life have programmed us in various ways. What we think, feel, and do are often associated with our lived experiences. Our thoughts and beliefs are often the results of how we have been programmed, have programmed ourselves and how we consistently continue to get programmed by the messages in society. Consider the messages you get every day from others and from yourself. Many people have been programmed throughout their lives by the people they have grown up with. Unfortunately, part of this programming involves the messages we received from negative influences in our lives. Changing the coding to our programmed minds will take a lot of time. The default negative programming causes negative emotional consequences. The negative programming or coding is like the Shovel Thoughts, and the positive programming or coding is the Ladder Thoughts.

## Baker

A metaphor that almost everyone can relate to involves food. When baking a cake, having a list of ingredients and steps associated with a recipe and process tends to make the baking experience easier. The identification and process of developing Ladder Thoughts is like having a recipe. That helps you to better prepare and address the Shovel Thoughts that interfere with your life. Additionally, the more you use the ladder Thought recipe, the easier it becomes, and the less time you need to actually look at the paper. Instead, the recipe and process start to work on memory and on habit. The same applies to Ladder Thought development and application in which the more you do it, the easier it becomes.

**Homework**

For your homework, grab your journal and just sit for about 10 minutes thinking about what type of analogy or metaphor may work better for you. Explore the examples provided, think of others you know, and use things that relate to you. Reflect on these things and write your thoughts down. If you do identify a different analogy or metaphor, what would you call the Ladder Thoughts? What would you call the Shovel Thoughts? Write it all down and consider personalizing your own growth by using the terms and concepts that fit you best.

# CHAPTER 8

# PUTTING IT ALL TOGETHER

You have learned all the different components and steps associated with the Ladder Thought process to counter Shovel Thoughts. Let's put it into action! Action is one of the most difficult things to do when it comes to change. For example, by now a significant portion of society realizes that eating certain foods and staying physically active will improve overall physical health and longevity. However, a significant number of people remain obese with resulting negative health consequences.

Many people have learned that spending within our means while saving for emergencies and retirement is a way toward a sustainable and more enjoyable life and retirement, often significantly reducing financial distress. However, many people still live beyond their means. I'm not faulting anyone for their physical or financial health as I realize change is difficult; however, knowledge paired with action is what helps change happen.

The call to action for the Ladder Thought process would involve doing the homework outlined throughout the book on a regular basis. Here is a to do list:

1) Write down what happened along with your Shovel Thoughts, and identify the kind of Shovel Thought and the unpleasant emotional experience.

2) Write down the Ladder Thought while identifying the type of Ladder Thought (i.e., **D.E.W.**).

3) Read the Ladder Thought repeatedly to assist in

shifting your thinking and resulting emotional reaction to a more positive cognitive and emotional state.

As I tell my clients, reading an instructional manual will provide you with knowledge; applying the knowledge will make you wise. Watching an exercise DVD at home while eating ice cream will not help anyone change their physical health status. The work in this process comes from actioning the steps to building Ladder Thoughts.

## Writing it Out

When writing out the situations, Shovel Thoughts and Ladder Thoughts hold tremendous value. You are not only thinking about it (cognitive) but are also writing it out (experiential/physical) and then reading it (visual). You allow yourself room to reflect and to focus on the process. When individuals try to jump into applying the process solely in their heads, they usually report feeling frustrated as the Shovel Thoughts can be so ingrained that the Ladder Thoughts have no chance. However, when they write it out, the Ladder Thoughts not only have a more significant impact but also a more lasting impact on the individual. There is a homework guide in Appendix A that can help you with an enhanced format. Get your journal that you have been using while reading this book and keep writing!

## Consistency

When it comes to change, consistency is probably one of the most important factors. Taking action toward a new goal on a regular basis is a key ingredient for change. When I work with clients, I tend to ask them to complete different instruments or checklists to gather an objective measure of their current clinical presentation. Many of these instruments have a Likert-type scale where 1 means "never," 2 means "rarely," 3 means "sometimes," etc. I get asked "how many times is 'sometimes' and how many times is 'often'?

To help you clarify what *rarely, sometimes,* and *often* mean to you, consider the following exercise:

1) If I ate a salad one day a week, how would you classify that frequency: a) Rarely; b) Sometimes; c) Often.

2) If I ate a salad two days a week, how would you classify that frequency: a) Rarely; b) Sometimes; c) Often.
3) If I ate a salad three days a week, how would you classify that frequency: a) Rarely; b) Sometimes; c) Often.
4) If I ate a salad four days a week, how would you classify that frequency: a) Rarely; b) Sometimes; c) Often.
5) If I ate a salad five days a week, how would you classify that frequency: a) Rarely; b) Sometimes; c) Often.

You get the idea. Take some time to classify a frequency into *rarely, sometimes* and *often*. You can even explore multiple times a day to meet your own definitions of these words. Our past and sensitivity to certain things can also impact what we consider to be *rarely, sometimes* and *often*. Lastly, our past and sensitivity to things influence how much certain situations impact us cognitively and emotionally.

For the purpose of the Ladder Thought homework, I will provide the following guidelines: Write out the process (i.e., situation, feeling, Shovel Thought, and Ladder Thought) for at least 50% of situations in which you felt something you did not want to feel (or) at least four (4) times a day, for at least five (5) days a week. Everyone is different, and some individuals may benefit from much more while others may need less. The guideline provided is not a magical formula but a starting guide toward one concept of consistency.

**Prepare**

Consider reflecting on your past to explore how you might have used a Ladder Thought in those situations. The Ladder Thoughts based on past experiences will provide you with prepared Ladder Thoughts to apply to similar situations in the future. Make note if you notice themes and patterns with your thought processes to increase awareness of the Shovel Thoughts that tend to be most present in your life. As another metaphor mentioned in Chapter 7 regarding the House on Fire, consider having "Extinguisher Thoughts" prepared for when the "Fire Thoughts" occur. Consider that knowing where the extinguisher is and how to get to it and use it can help minimize the damage of a fire, especially if you catch it early. Having these pre-scripted, prepared Ladder Thoughts (or Extinguisher Thoughts) can help you quickly address the Shovel Thought (or Fire Thought) and reduce the amount and duration of distress.

## Share

One of the lessons I've learned in life is that the more I talk about something the better I tend to understand the topic. Therefore, I try to present regularly on topics of interest to me from a professional standpoint but also talk to others about non-mental health topics (I'm obsessed with economics, investing, etc.). My wonderful wife listens to countless scenarios in which I'm sharing what I learned about in a book, podcast, or video regarding mental health, financial education, economics, or investing. While she may glean information from my sharing, I'm the one who more greatly reaps the benefit. As I talk and think about these topics, the more I understand them. Therefore, I would like to invite you to find someone you trust and tell them about your Shovel Thoughts and how you used Ladder Thoughts to counteract them. Share with them how you were able to cut down the amount of time you felt sad and how you learned to focus your energy on what you can do to change your situation. Explain how you were able to forgive someone and relieve yourself of that pain. Explain how you used parts of the **D.E.W.** Ladder Thought process to walk through different challenges. The more you talk about how and what you did, the more ingrained it will become, resulting in you becoming more and more of a Ladder Thoughts master.

## Farewell

Now that you have completed this guide to emotional change, it is time to put it into practice. Use the strategies you have learned throughout your day for big and small situations. The more you practice and refer to this book, the better you will become at implementing the strategies naturally throughout your day and life.

# APPENDIX A - HELPFUL TOOLS AND RESOURCES

### 1. Shovel Thought Quiz

The Shovel Thought quiz is presented to help you better identify what types of Shovel Thoughts are more prevalent in your life. Please respond to each statement by circling either "yes" or "no." Circle "yes" if you believe that the statement tends to be like you. No one statement will be 100% or always like you, so please be open to considering each statement and if it tends to fit you. Instead of seeing the "yes" or "no" as All-or-Nothing, for the purpose of this exercise, answer which one best defines you (i.e., that would explain your reaction most of the time).

1. I get upset if things don't go the way I planned.
    Yes        No

2. I think about bad things happening to people I care about.
    Yes        No

3. I enjoy spending time with others.
    Yes        No

4. I think that bad things always happen to me.
    Yes        No

5. I tend to emotionally and psychologically beat myself up when something does not work out.
    Yes        No

6. I try to show appreciation for things/actions people do for me.
    Yes          No

7. Problems are usually not my fault.
    Yes          No

8. Most people don't do what they are supposed to.
    Yes          No

9. I need to think about all the bad things that can happen, so that I can do something about it.
    Yes          No

10. I wake up every morning and think, "What can I do today to make someone I care about happy"?
    Yes          No

11. If I get into an argument with someone, it is probably because they did something to start it.
    Yes          No

12. I never get my way.
    Yes          No

13. If people do what they are supposed to, then things would work out fine.
    Yes          No

14. I want to improve my relationship with others and know that I need to change things to make that happen.
    Yes          No

15. If I'm not happy, it is usually because of what someone else did.
    Yes          No

16. If something bad happens, I know that there are more bad things right around the corner.
    Yes          No

17. If I get into an argument with someone, it is probably my fault.
   Yes        No

18. I am willing to compromise with others in order to get along better and have a better relationship with them.
   Yes        No

19. I know when things are going to get bad based on what others say or do.
   Yes        No

20. People always disappointment me.
   Yes        No

21. It is my fault if things don't work out.
   Yes        No

22. I care about people in my life and will do whatever it takes to make things work.
   Yes        No

23. If someone does not show up on time, I tend to think that something horrible happened.
   Yes        No

24. I can tell when an argument is going to occur between me and others.
   Yes        No

25. There are a lot of bad things that can happen, and I find myself thinking about them.
   Yes        No

26. I look forward to spending time with people I care about.
   Yes        No

27. When I think about the hard times in my life, I tend to think about all the things I should have done differently.
    Yes        No

28. I find it hard not to think about worst-case scenarios.
    Yes        No

29. When something bad happens, I can already see someone else starting to get ready to argue before they even say anything.
    Yes        No

30. I daydream about the wonderful times I've spent with others.
    Yes        No

Once you have completed the quiz, look at the item numbers below to help you identify what Shovel thoughts you tend to experience most. You may find yourself having some within all the categories or more in other categories. This is just a quick guide to help you better identify your thought patterns.

Expectation Shovel Thoughts: Items numbered: 1,8,13

My Fault Shovel Thoughts: Items numbered: 5,17,21,27

Worst-Case Shovel Thoughts: Items numbered: 2, 23,28

All-or-Nothing Shovel Thoughts: Items numbered: 4,12,20

And Then/What If Shovel Thoughts: Items numbered: 9,16,25

Here We Go Again Shovel Thoughts: Items numbered: 19,24,29

Blaming Shovel Thoughts: Items numbered: 7,11,15

Positive Interpersonal Thoughts: Items numbered: 3,6,10,14,18,22,26,30

## 2. Feelings Worksheet

This worksheet is designed to help you identify the types of Shovel Thoughts you have had that are usually associated with the different emotions listed. First, write out a Shovel Thought that you have had in the past that led you to feeling the emotion identified. If you can't think of a specific Shovel Thought, then think of a time or situation in which you felt that emotion, and then identify what Shovel Thought may have been associated with the emotion. Use your journal to really expand on this process and keep adding to it when you identify other Shovel Thoughts that come up.

1) Sad

_____
_____
_____
_____
_____
_____
_____

2) Angry

_____
_____
_____
_____
_____
_____
_____

3) Lonely

_____
_____
_____
_____
_____
_____
_____

4) Disappointed

5) Guilty

6) Worried/Anxious

7) Frustrated

Did you notice any themes in terms of Shovel Thought patterns? Use the information from this exercise to help improve your awareness of specific types of Shovel Thoughts that may trigger these emotional reactions.

### 3. The Remainder of the Serenity Prayer:

*"God, grant me the serenity to accept the things I cannot change, Courage to change the things I can, and the wisdom to know the difference. Living one day at a time; Enjoying one moment at a time; accepting hardship as a pathway to peace. Taking, as He did, this sinful world as it is, not as I would have it. Trusting that He will make all things right if I surrender to His Will; That I may be reasonably happy in this life, and supremely happy with Him forever in the next. Amen."* (Reinhold Niebuhr).

### 4. Homework Guide:

1) What happened? _____

_____

_____

2) How did you feel? _____

On a scale of 1 to 10 with 1 being mild and 10 being extreme, how strong was the feeling? _____

3) What was your Shovel thought (and what type of Shovel Thought was it)?

_____

_____

_____

_____

4) Develop a Ladder thought.

D.E.W. – What would be a helpful Ladder Thought?

_____
_____
_____
_____
_____
_____
_____

5) Did you have a different emotional state after applying the Ladder Thought? _____

If yes, what was the different emotion?

_____

If no, did the intensity of the emotion you felt change any (refer to the scale of 1 to 10 in step 2)? ____

If yes, to what number? _____

# ABOUT THE AUTHOR

 Christian J. Dean, Ph.D. is licensed as a professional counselor (LPC) and a Marriage and Family Therapist (LMFT) in Louisiana, where he practices at Counseling for Growth, LLC. He has put into practice the tenants of this book with clients for over 15 years. His focus on action and change are at the forefront of his practice. Dr. Dean is also a Clinical Faculty member in the Clinical Mental Health Counseling Program at Southern New Hampshire University.

www.ingramcontent.com/pod-product-compliance
Lightning Source LLC
Chambersburg PA
CBHW032131090426
42743CB00007B/561